Written by

Dr. Ma. Rosario S. Racho

Illustrated by

Maria Soledad S. Racho

Meow and Furever: Growing Up With Your Cat

Text copyright © 2017 Dr. Ma. Rosario Racho
Illustrations copyright © 2017 Maria Soledad Racho
Published in 2017 by St. Matthew's Publishing Corporation (through its imprint Kahel Press)
Publishers since 1989, with nationwide operations in the Philippines
for the distribution of educational books and children's books.

Editor: Ruth Valorie Catabijan
Layout Artist: Maria Soledad Racho

First Edition: October 2017

ISBN: 978-971-625-371-9

How to Order
Purchase individual copies from: https://shopee.ph/st.matthewspublishing

Copies are also available at special rates in bulk orders. Contact the publisher through the details below.

St. Matthew's Publishing Corporation
First RVC Building, 92 Anonas Cor. K-6th Streets, East Kamias, Quezon City
(02) 8426-5611 || inquiry@stmatthews.ph
www.stmatthews.ph

Dedicated to my first cat ever, Marble, wherever you might be,
and my eight other cats namely, Miumiu, Blue,
Pepper, Bubbles, Emu, Neko, Calico, and Pebo.
May you all grow up healthy with me~

Special mention to my oldest Siamese cat, Chewy,
whose kitty soul is well-rested and happy.

Preface

Pet care books haven't always been available in the market and if they are, most of these would be text heavy. The idea of this handy book is to deliver its relevant contents in a simplified manner which would help both kids and adults easily understand how to take care of their cats.

This book was also written in order to break common misconceptions and/or myths that many people may know about cats. From my experience as a veterinarian, they are only a few people that I know of who have cats as their pets. It may be because many people say that cats are hard to take care of and are not as sweet as dogs, which has been always called a man's best friend. This is quite untrue. Because of the lack of proper knowledge of how cats behave and how to take care of them, they are easily misunderstood.

Flipping through the chapters, you'll gain a better understanding of cats. It is highly advised that you read the book in an orderly manner, starting from Chapter 1 onwards. However, all chapters are written independently, with a few references on other chapters, and can be used as a guide.

Majority of the contents on this book are based on my personal experience and knowledge as a veterinarian and as a cat owner. It is helpful that I understand my cats in both points-of- view and that I get to share to you, the readers, my experiences and knowledge.

<u>CAT PROFILE</u>

CAT'S NAME: ____

BIRTHDAY: ____

BREED: ____

MALE/FEMALE: ____

COLOR/MARKINGS: ____

DATE ACQUIRED: ____

THIS BOOKS BELONGS TO:

(YOUR NAME) ____

IF FOUND, PLEASE BRING BACK TO:

(ADDRESS) ____

____

OR CALL:

(PHONE NUMBERS) ____

____

PLACE PICTURE/S OF YOUR CAT HERE

TABLE OF CONTENTS

Chapter 1

WHAT IS A CAT?
An Introduction to Cats

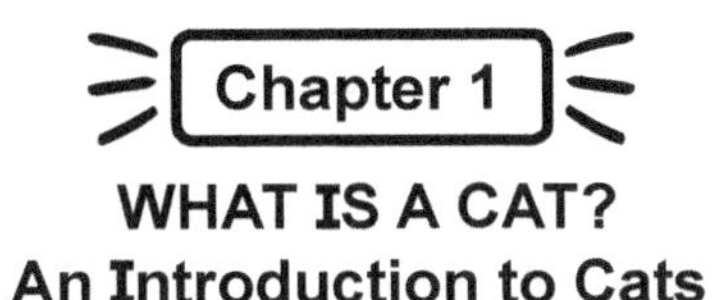

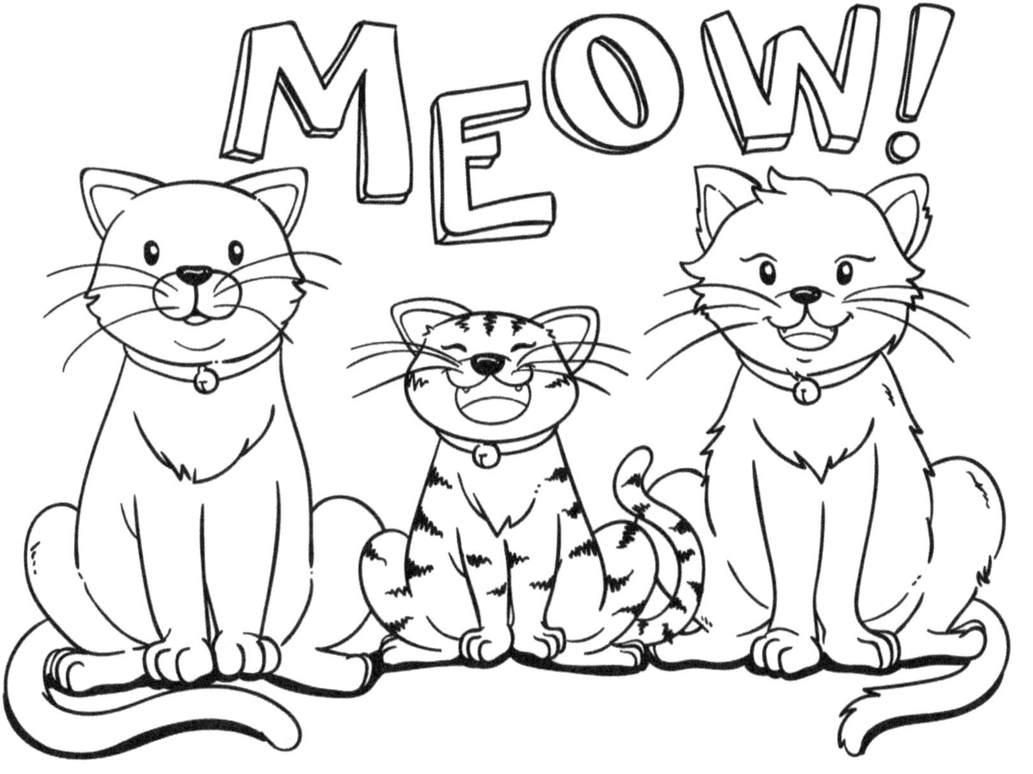

Many people think that cats are aloof or unfriendly creatures. They may think that cats do not make good pets and are less friendly than dogs. This is not true. Cats are cute and cuddly pets. They are more independent as compared to dogs but can be as sweet as them.

It is not simple to take care of a cat but it is a FUN responsibility.

SHORT HISTORY

Having a cat at home is now becoming more common. People might ask, *"Where do cats come from?"*

Cats have been domesticated way later than dogs. They have a very interesting history throughout the years.

It started several thousand years back in ancient Egypt. Cats are highly respected and worshipped by Egyptians during this era. They helped a lot with the Egyptians' wealth and success by protecting the Egyptians' crops from pests such as mice and rats. Cats also hunted venomous snakes that kept the Egyptians safe. Because of these traits, the Egyptians believed that cats brought good luck to their community and had begun worshipping them.

However, the Christian church did not agree with cats being worshipped. It was during this time when rumors spread that black cats brought bad luck and was usually associated with witchcraft.

Humans later realized that cats are actually helpful regardless of their color and shape. More people have been taking care of cats as their pets and have been treating them as part of their family.

CATS ARE GREAT PETS, TOO!

Cats make great companions mainly because of their independence. They are also very clean, cuddly and quiet most of the time.

They don't require big spaces to live in. They are quite comfortable in small spaces.

The average life span of a cat is about 13-15 years old. The length of their stay with their families would depend on how the owners, their families, take care and understand them very well.

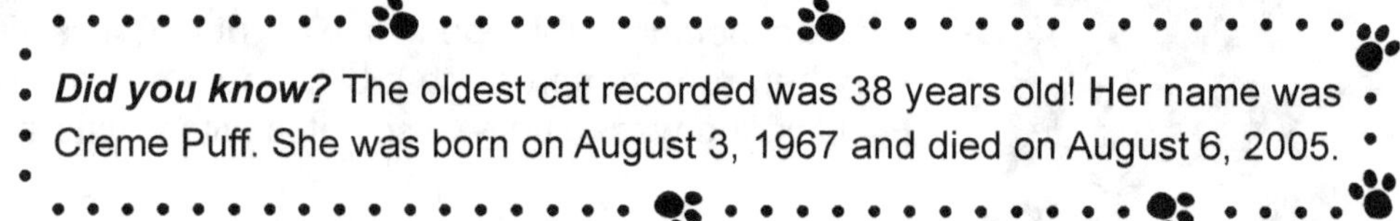

Did you know? The oldest cat recorded was 38 years old! Her name was Creme Puff. She was born on August 3, 1967 and died on August 6, 2005.

Before taking a new cat home, there are a few things that you need to consider. Be sure that all members of the family are ready for the responsibility and are capable to raise a cat.

It is best for the family to understand the cat very well from its needs to its wants, and start reading this book as a guide.

Chapter 2

THE DEVELOPING CAT

The Different Life Stages of a Cat

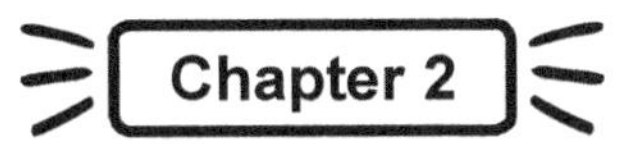

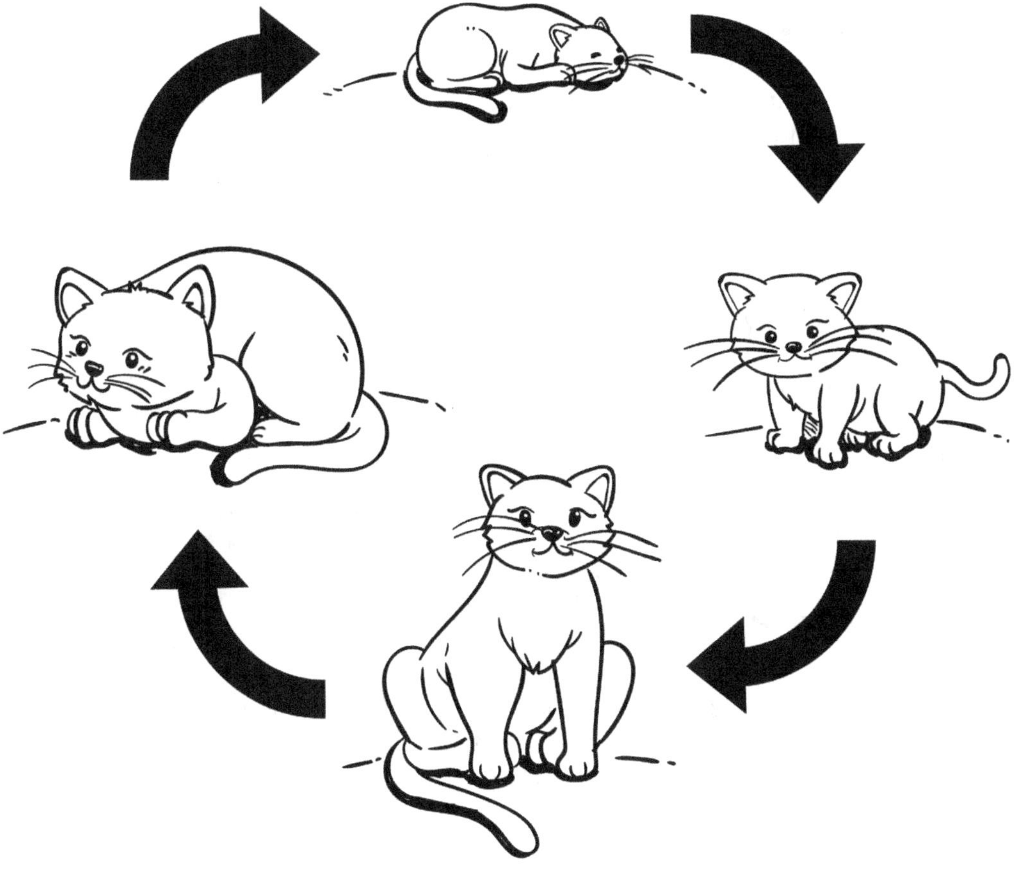

NEWBORN CATS AND KITTENS

Newborn cats are very fragile creatures. They cannot eat, drink, urinate and poop on their own and are very dependent on their mother cat.

When the baby cats or kittens are born, their initial instinct is to look for their mother and suck milk. It is important that the kittens drink their mother's milk for the first 24 hours because the first milk that the mother produces, which is called the colostrum, is highly nutritious for kittens.

Kittens are frequent feeders and will drink milk from their mother almost every one to two hours. A kitten will suck milk from its mother even after 2 months of age but this may become already painful for the mother because of the kitten's teeth. To help its mother, wet feeding for the kittens can be started at around 3 weeks of age.

Kittens under two weeks of age depend on stimulus to urinate and poop on their own. The mother cat will lick its kittens' genitals and anus to stimulate urination and defecation, respectively. This is usually done by the mother cat a few minutes after the kittens had already drank milk from her.

Kittens are born with their eyes closed. Their eyes only open around two weeks of age but they cannot see yet at this time. They will only start seeing their surroundings at around three to four weeks of age.

Because kittens are very fragile and sensitive, intensive care is much needed. You, as its new owner, have to take responsibility for it just like its mother cat.

Check **Chapter 11** for ideas on how to take care of adopted/abandoned cats.

ADULT CATS

Adult cats are the easiest to take care of among the cat's life stages. This is because they are already very independent at this stage.

Feeding an adult cat is easy but some cats may be picky. There is a wide range of food choices to be given to an adult cat. See **Chapter 5** for more details regarding this.

<u>Mating</u>

Female cats will attract male cats at around 6 months of age. Do not panic when your female cat starts to become more talkative and noisy during this age. This is normal to them and it is what we call **heat** or when a cat is **in heat**.

Cats in heat may *meow* non-stop to attract and call on male cats. They become sensitive to your touch and are extra affectionate. They will rub their bodies more often on different furniture and the floor.

The female cat in heat may also freeze with constant touching thinking that a male cat would start mating it. This cycle may last for about a week and may occur every one to two months if the cat does not become pregnant.

Male cats, on the other hand, can sense if a female cat is in heat and will look for it through smell and hearing.

If several males are near the female cat in heat, they might fight over the female cat and can cause serious injuries among themselves.

If you have a multiple-cat household with both male and female cats, it is highly recommended to **neuter** the cats to avoid unwanted pregnancies and serious injuries. (See **Chapter 10** to know more about **neutering**).

In addition, if you have a female cat in heat at home, male stray cats may visit outside your home since they can sense your female cat from the outside.

Pregnancy

Your female cat will become pregnant if it has successfully mated with a male cat. Your cat may only look fat during the first part of its pregnancy and you will slowly observe its tummy becoming bigger. Its mammary glands may also look swollen with milk discharge.

Cat pregnancy is about 60-65 days. If your cat is starting to hide in a darker isolated room and starts pawing, she may be about to give birth. Most cats can deliver their babies alone but assistance by a veterinarian may be needed if the cat is not yet giving birth for about 5 hours after isolation and observation of watery discharge from the vulva.

SENIOR CATS

Senior or old cats need as much attention as kittens. They are also as fragile as kittens. Senior cats are less active and are more prone to aging diseases such as kidney problems—the reason why careful attention to its food and activities is needed.

Restriction with its food choices such as a lower protein in its food might be necessary. Stressful activities should also be minimal to avoid injuries.

Dealing with the death of a cat

The death of a cat is like a death of a family member or a friend. This can be very painful, so grieve if you must. Do not contain your feelings inside and find some support among other members of your family and friends. Remember the good memories that your cat has with you and your family, and know that your cat may be in a good place after death.

There are several ways to rest your dead cat's body at peace. Some would bury them within the owner's backyard or in a pet cemetery. Others would like to have their cats cremated and then placed in an urn for safe-keeping.

There are several veterinary clinics that are associated with pet cemeteries and cremation services. You may inquire with your veterinarian if they know any pet cemetery or cremation services within your area.

If you want to get a new cat, it is best to consult your veterinarian about getting one especially if your cat died from an illness. Certain bacteria or viruses that may have caused your former cat's illness has to be fully eradicated first from your home before getting a new cat.

Chapter 3

WELCOME HOME, KITTY!
What to Do and to Prepare for Your New Cat

Bringing a new cat to your home is like entering an unknown world for them. Everything will be new to them and this can be stressful to your cat. It is important to make your cat feel at home so that it will not be scared to enter the house.

Your cat might have to adjust slowly with its new home—YOUR HOME. When the cat enters the new home for the first time, do not let too many people touch and interact with it yet. You do not want to scare it.

If you have another pet before your new cat, isolate the new cat first for about **one week**. If the cat is healthy and you do not observe any disease, slowly let it interact with your other pets.

Some cats can be friendly with dogs and other cats even during their first meeting but most of them would have to get used to them slowly.

To help your cat easily adapt to the new home, ask the previous owner or the owner of the pet store where you got your cat what specific brands and materials the cat has been using for its everyday routine.

Before getting a new cat, make sure that you are prepared for everything. You should already have all the supplies you need, and your family should also be ready for the responsibility.

WHAT YOU NEED:

- ☐ Bed
- ☐ Litter box and scoop
- ☐ Litter sand
- ☐ Cat food and treats
- ☐ Food and water bowls
- ☐ Carrier or cage
- ☐ Collar
- ☐ Harness
- ☐ Toys
- ☐ Scratch post
- ☐ Cleaning supplies

BED

To keep your cat warm and cozy especially when it sleeps, it needs a comfortable bed just like you. If you want your cat to be your roommate, its bed can be placed in one corner of your bedroom and away from the food and water bowls, and its litter box. If your cat does not use its bed at first, observe where your cat wants to sleep during its first few days in your home. It may be a darker or quieter part of your room/house. You may place the bed in this area instead.

There are several types of beds that you can buy or prepare for your cat. Cat beds that are commonly available in the market are the open-type and enclosed ones. Some cats can be picky with their beds, while some are not. Cats that prefer a quieter and isolated place when sleeping will choose an enclosed type over the open-type bed.

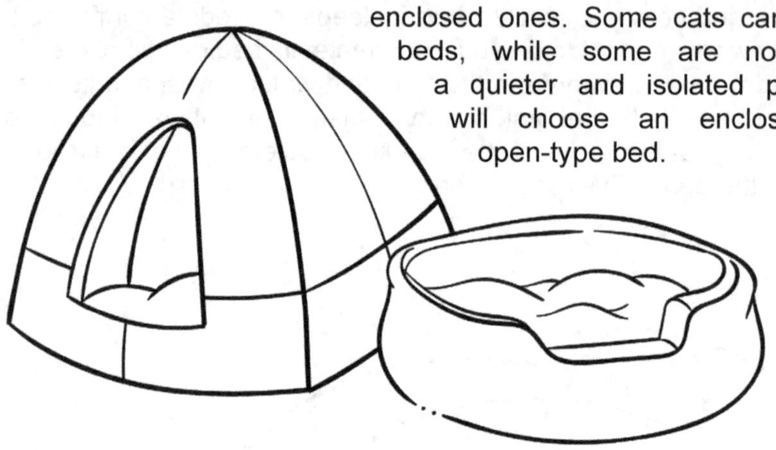

Make sure that the bed or its beddings are easy to wash. It has to be washed regularly to remove dirt that may accumulate over time.

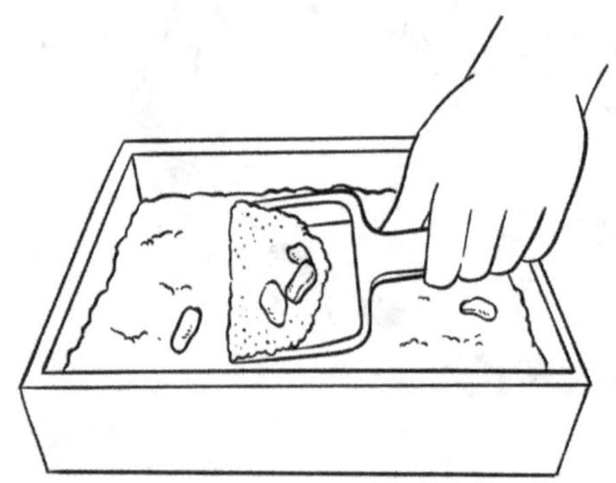

LITTER BOX, SAND AND SCOOP

Cats are very clean creatures and they don't want their beds and other play areas to be dirty. When they poo and urinate, they will attempt to cover these to protect themselves from predators that may smell their urine. This is a behaviour they got from their ancestors.

If you intend to let your cat stay indoors, a litter box is a must! Provide one litter box per cat and always have an extra litter box inside your house especially if you have multiple cats. For example, if you have three (3) cats at home, four (4) litter boxes should be provided. This will allow your cat to naturally manifest its territorial behaviour. (See **Chapter 8** to know more about cat's **territorial** behaviour.) It is advisable that you use a litter box that is easy to clean like one that is of a plastic material.

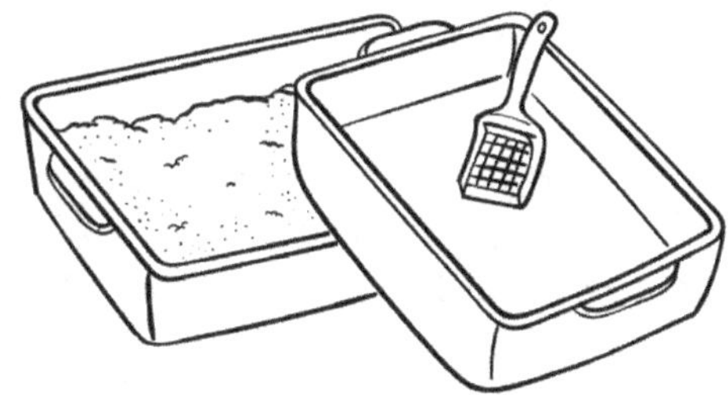

There are several types of litter material that you can use for your cat. Some may even have scents to cover the smell of their poop and urine.

Litter material may also be clumping or non-clumping to easily detect if your cat has already pooped and urinated. Clumping material can be easily removed from the remaining untouched litter material inside the box.

Another characteristic that can be considered when choosing a litter material is if it is organic or not. Most organic litter material can be buried in soil to be added for fertilizer or flushed into toilets.

Below are the types of litter material you can choose from.

Litter sand with advantage and disadvantage

SAND

most clumping of all, easier to clean-up,
non-flushable in toilet, reasonably priced

Organic pellet material (corn)

clumping, can be buried in soil for fertilizer,
flushable in toilet, can be expensive

HUSK, wood shreds

non-clumping, more difficult to clean up if with urine,
can be buried in soil for fertilizer, non-flushable in
toilet, cheapest

There are a few things to consider when preparing and cleaning your cat's litter box. See **Chapter 7** on how to prepare and clean your cat's litter box. A litter scoop is also needed to easily pick up the clumps from the litter box.

Cats will instinctively know how to use a litter box because of their innate hygienic nature. However, kittens may need a little assistance for this routine but they can also learn from their mother. Kittens may start using the litter box at about one month of age. To know more about how to train your cat to use a litter box, see **Chapter 7**.

CAT FOOD AND TREATS

Cat food is the main source of your cat's nutrients and energy. It is important to be familiar with what your cat has to eat and what it cannot eat.

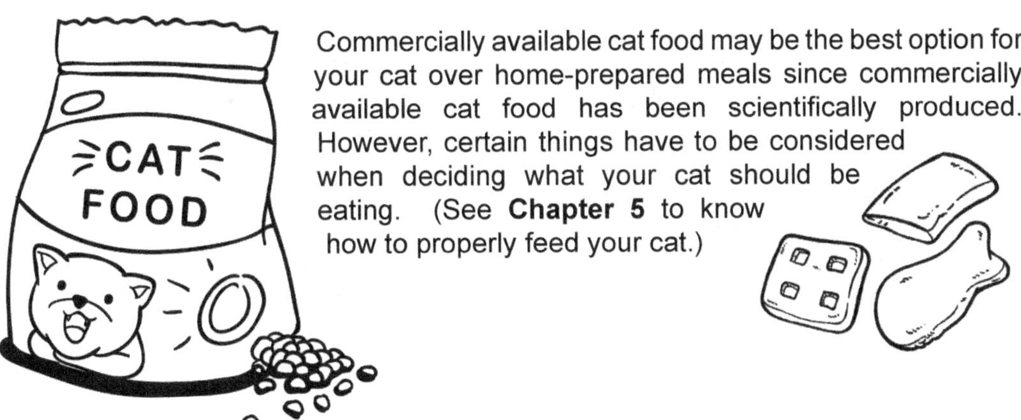

Commercially available cat food may be the best option for your cat over home-prepared meals since commercially available cat food has been scientifically produced. However, certain things have to be considered when deciding what your cat should be eating. (See **Chapter 5** to know how to properly feed your cat.)

FOOD AND WATER BOWLS

It is essential to place your cat's food and water bowl in a constant place or position as part of their routine. This will train your cat to eat at one place only.

Food and water bowls can be made from different materials such as plastic, ceramic, and stainless steel which should be easy to clean. Regardless of the material, the water bowl has to be bigger than your food bowl to allow your cat to drink more.

CARRIER AND CAGE

Carriers and cages are helpful especially when you bring your cat to the veterinarian or when simply traveling. It has to be fully secured since cats are good escape artists. The cage or carrier should have small openings or holes to prevent your cat from suffocating inside. Carrier and cage windows should be minimal in size because cats may panic when they are too exposed outside and they see that they are in an unfamiliar place.

COLLAR AND HARNESS

Collars, together with name tags, may serve as an identification for your cat especially if it has access outside. The tag may include the owner's name, address and/or contact number.

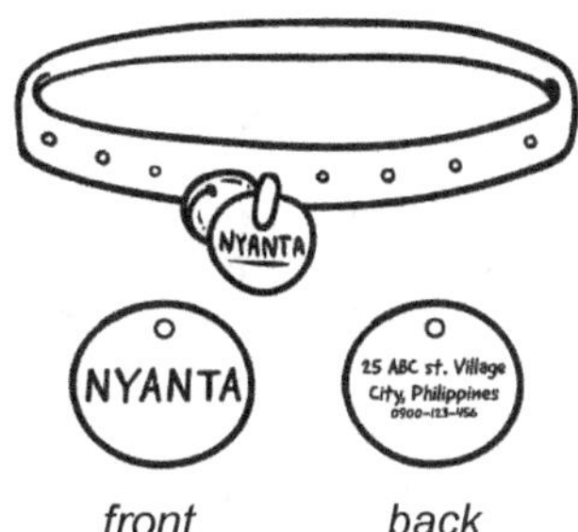

front   *back*

Some owners put a bell on the collar instead of a tag. This will help them to easily locate their cat inside the house because the bell makes a sound every time the cat moves.

If you use a bell, always check if it is securely attached to the collar. Some cats may play with the bell and accidentally remove them. If the bell is removed from the collar, it is possible that your cat may swallow it.

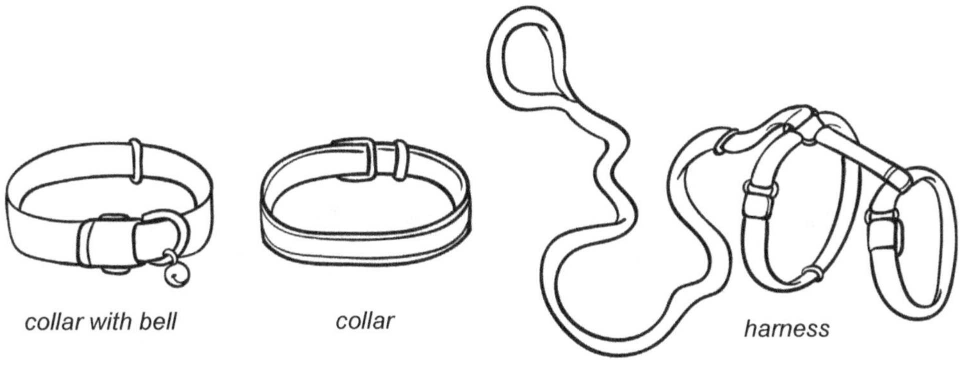

collar with bell   *collar*   *harness*

Make sure that the collar is not too loose and not too tight on your cat's neck. If the collar is too loose, the collar can be easily removed from the cat's neck. If the collar is too tight, your cat might choke and may also have difficulty in breathing and swallowing. You should be able to fit 2-3 fingers loosely between the collar and your cat's neck.

CAT TOYS AND PLAY TIME

Cats, especially kittens, are just like kids. They love to play around. Playtime for cats serves as bonding time with you, their playmates and other cats.

Always play with your cat especially if it is the only pet in your home. Playing with it can make it smarter. It is also a good form of exercise for them.

Cats are easily attracted to movement and sound, and may play even with simple, random things such as paper, cloth and thread. Therefore, be careful with leaving small and sharp things behind that may injure your cat and be swallowed by your cat.

REMEMBER! Your cat is NOT THE TOY. Handle it gently with care. Rowdy handling may result in your cat biting you! Do not pull its tail at all times.

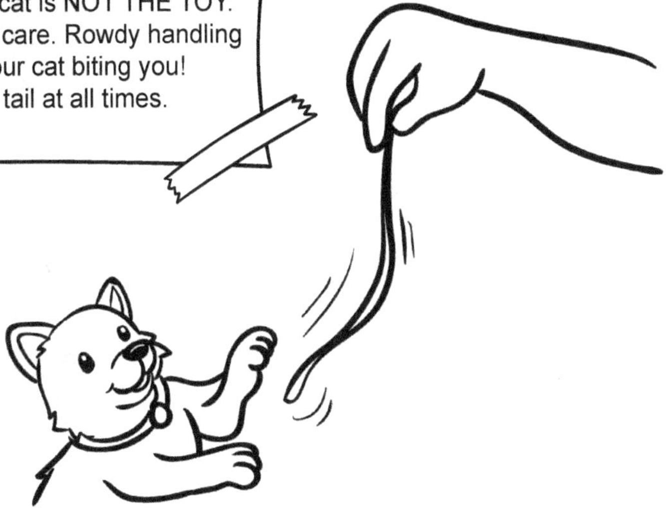

SCRATCHING POST

One of a cat's natural behaviours is scratching with its claws and paws on wood trunks, posts and the like. This behaviour helps them mark their territory and sharpen their claws.

When a cat stays indoors, its tendency is to look for furniture or anything inside the house where it can scratch its claws on.

Cats would normally try out a lot of furniture first before it picks out the one (or maybe two) furniture it feels best on its paws. The result of this behaviour is the destruction of these furniture.

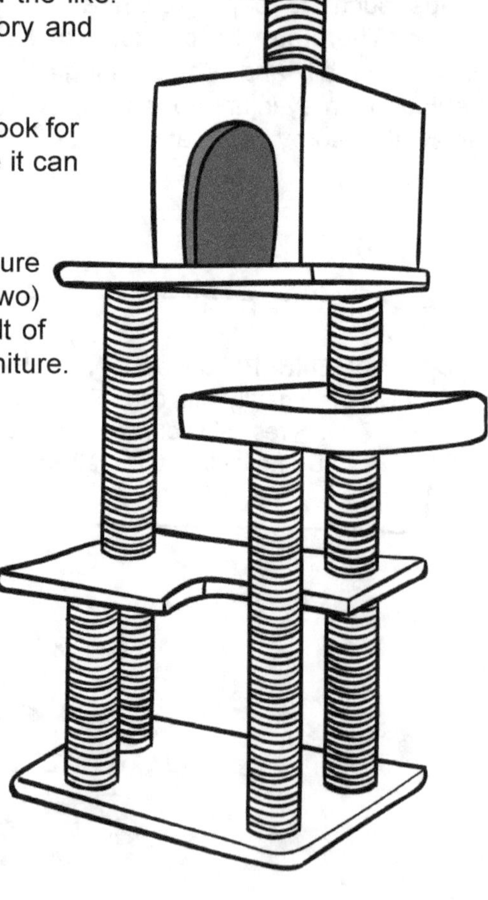

To avoid this, it is best to provide a scratch post for your cat. It should have a stable base and should be big enough for your cat to stretch on it. The scratching post material to choose could depend on what you have noticed your cat liked a lot. Commonly used materials are coconut husks, wood, carpet fabric, cardboard and ropes.

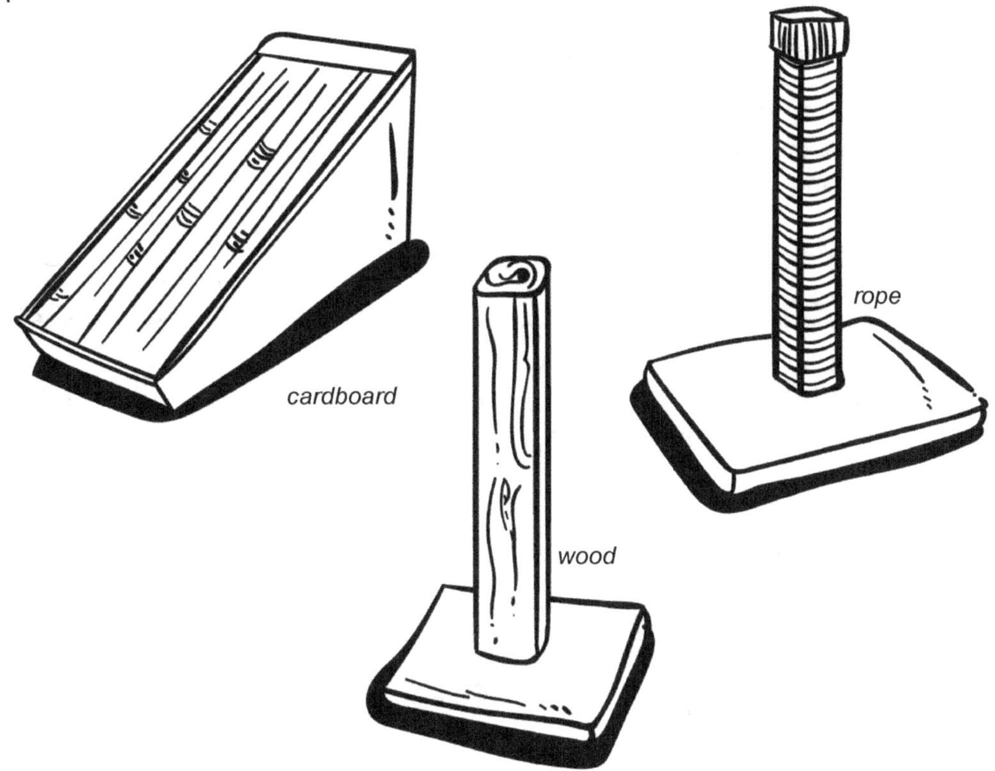

See **Chapter 4** on how to train your cat to use a scratching post.

CLEANING SUPPLIES

Keeping any pet in your home also means that an amount of mess is unavoidable. These messes can be as simple as urine outside the litter box when your cat hasn't been trained yet or as difficult as a vomit when your cat becomes sick. Be sure to have a number of cleaning materials to keep your house clean.

When cleaning these messes using cleaning agents such as bleach, be careful not to let your cat around the messy area to avoid itself from getting into contact or ingesting chemicals while you are cleaning.
You may also buy safer cleaning agents in pet stores and veterinary clinics. If you are unsure, ask your veterinarian what might be best to use.

Chapter 4

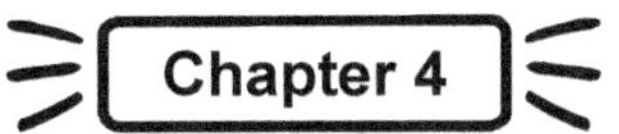

HOUSE PROTECTION PROGRAM

Cat-Proofing the House from Those Claws

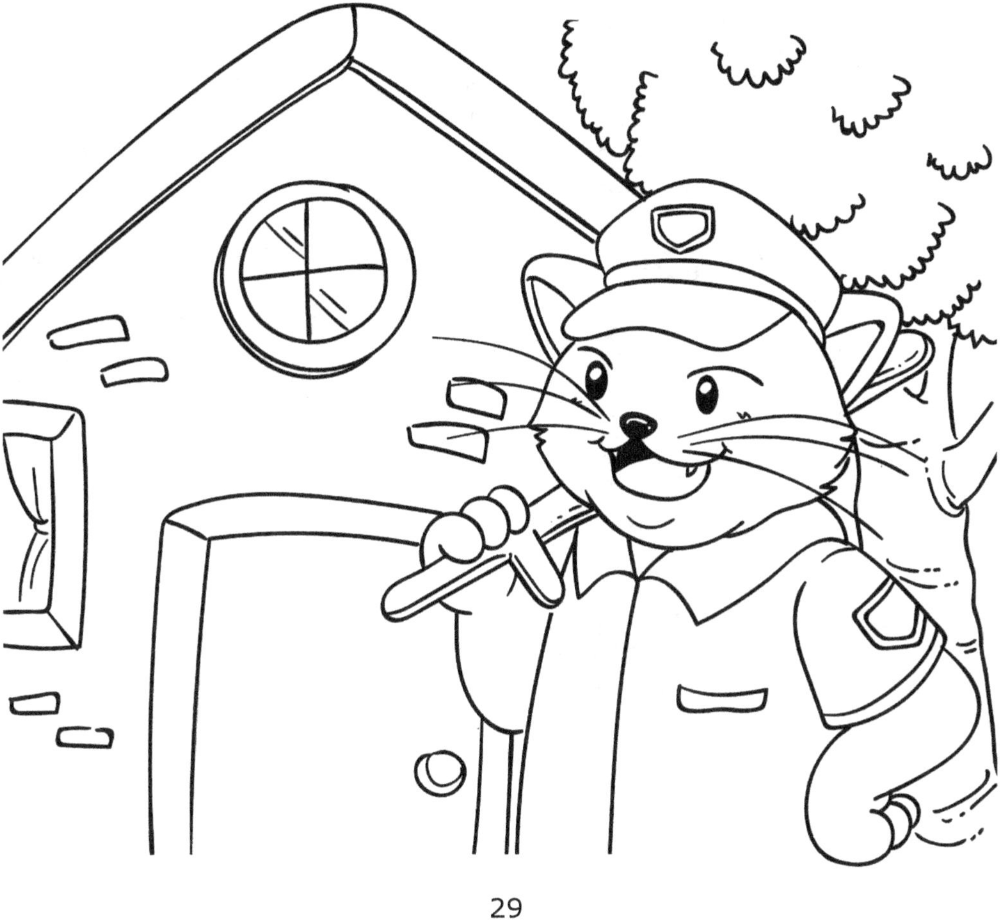

One of the most problematic behaviours that cat owners complain about is when cats like to scratch their claws on different furniture such as sofas and wooden table legs.

Owners would often call their cats destructive because of this. A simple solution to this problem is to provide your cat with a scratch post.

Scratching posts can easily be bought in pet stores. They are made from different materials (See page 26). Most cats would prefer a certain material over another. However, training your cat to get used to a certain scratching post can be done.

Teaching Your Cat to Use a Scratching Post:

1. Before training your cat to use the scratching post you bought for it, train your cat first not to scratch the furniture that your cat scratches on. You can do this my placing a bunch of sticky tapes on the furniture. The sticky feeling when your cat scratches the furniture will discourage it from using the furniture as a scratching material.

A simple tap on your cat's nose while saying "NO" can also do the trick when you want to discipline your cat into not using the furniture as a scratching post.

2. Make sure the scratching post's base is stable. Bring your cat near the scratching post. Let it smell the post at first. Adding catnip, which can be bought in pet stores, on the post will help encourage your cat to use the post.

3. Hold your cat's front legs and mimic the scratching behaviour it does on the scratching post. Make sure that its paws touch the scratch post itself.

4. Do this on a regular basis, at least twice a day, until your cat finally uses its own scratching post.

It is better to provide an extra scratching post for your cats especially if you have more than one cat at home. This is because cats can also become territorial with each scratching post.

Chapter 5

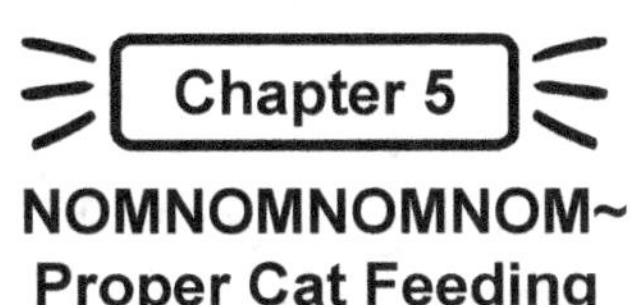

NOMNOMNOMNOM~ Proper Cat Feeding

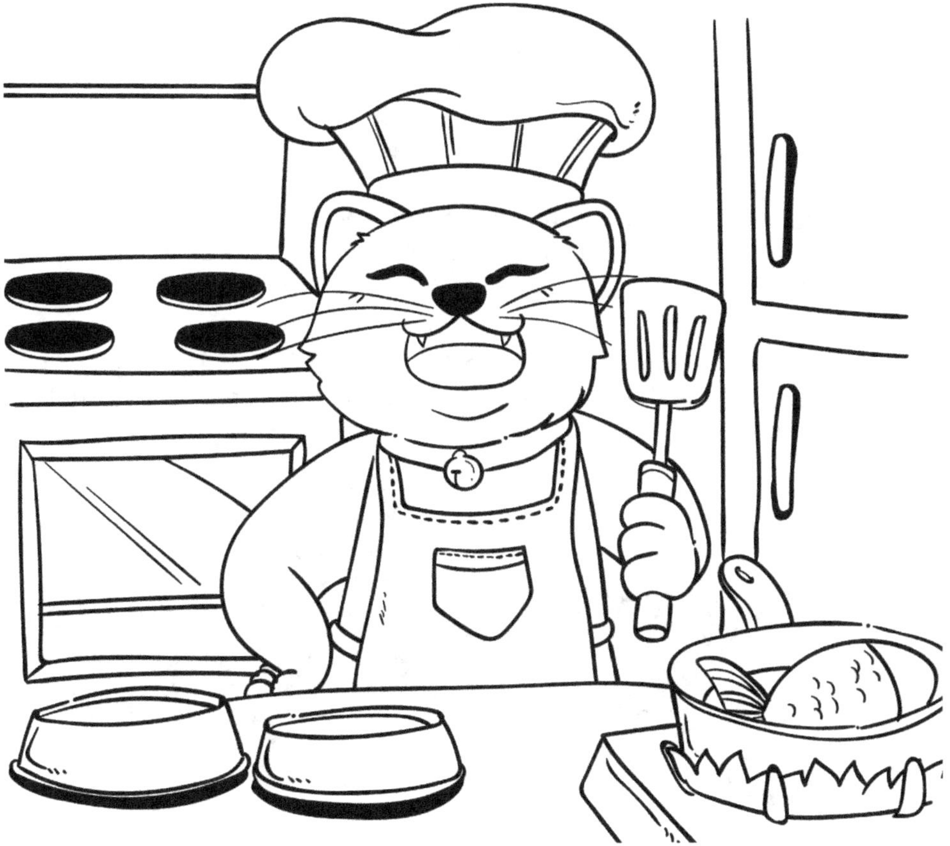

Your cat, unlike us humans, are carnivorous meaning their nutritional requirement is highly based on meat. Cats need many nutrients that can only be found in meat, not vegetables. Other sources of their nutrients are carbohydrates from grains or rice.

The cat's teeth, unlike dog's, was made for meat-eating. Feeding your cat with vegetables is not advised unless your cat has a disease/sickness that needs vegetables and fiber.

Kittens need more meals as compared to adults because of their hyperactive behaviour. You may follow the guide below on how frequent you will feed your cat.

Kittens – two to three times a day
Adults – one to two times a day

You have to give more food to your cat if it is more active and playful. The amount of food that you will give your cat will also depend if you are giving wet or dry food. More food is usually given if you give wet food.

Cats will also have a different eating and drinking behaviour depending on the season.

Summer or hot season – Less food intake, more water intake
Rainy or cold season – More food intake, less water intake

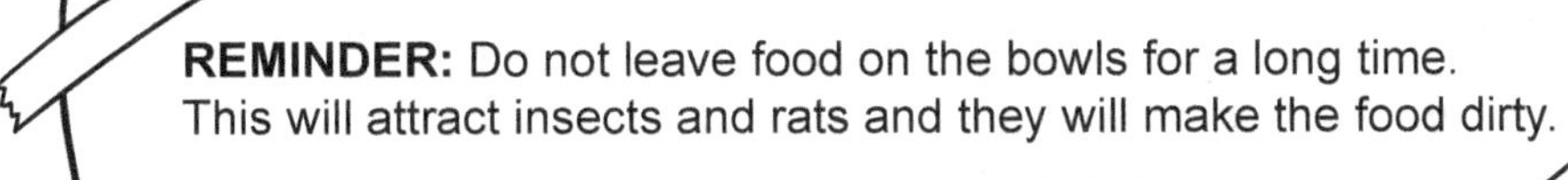

FOOD

Cat food may differ based on how the food was prepared and based on its water content. Any of the food types can be given to your cat. Just do not forget the age and activity of your cat. Kittens would need more protein as compared to adult cats.

Food type based on preparation :

<u>COMMERCIALLY-PRODUCED vs HOME-COOKED</u>

1. **Commercially available food**
   This food are the pellets and canned wet food with brands that you see in the market. They have different flavors and different types.

   Pellets have less water compared to canned wet food. That is why canned wet food may spoil easily if not stored properly.

   These food are scientifically produced for your cat to get all the nutrients it needs every day except for water. Complete nutritional needs are almost always provided by commercially available food.

When choosing what type or brand you'll give your pet, you can consider its price. Food with more quality may be more expensive because more studies were done to produce the better cat food.

> **SIDE NOTE:** You should avoid giving human canned food because it is salty and has a lot of preservatives.

2. Home-cooked food

Preparing home-cooked food for your cat is not an easy task because it can be time-consuming. However, it can be very fulfilling to you as the owner.

If you prefer to give this to your cat, discuss with your veterinarian regarding a recipe that you can use. Proper proportion of ingredients should be done to get the right amount of vitamins and minerals per day. See **Chapter 12** for recipes on home-cooked food for your cats.

Store your home-cooked food properly in a cold place (refrigerator or freezer). Do not add bones, if possible. Bones may become brittle when cooked. And when these bones break, they can become very sharp which may cause harm to your cat such as wounds on its mouth and trauma inside its stomach or intestines.

Below are examples of protein that you may use in your recipes.

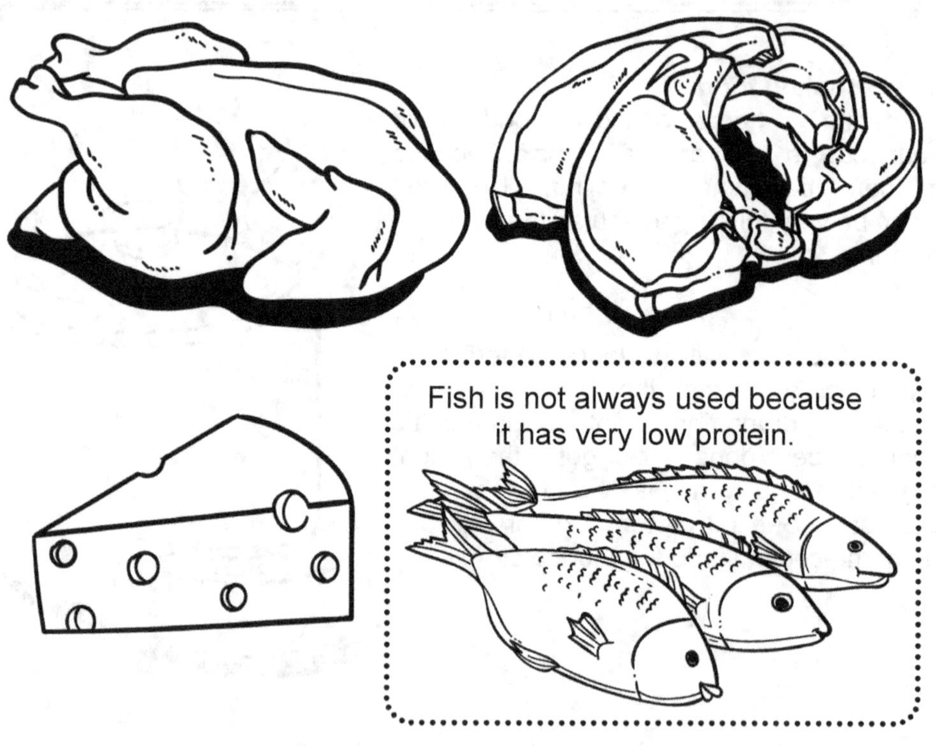

Food type based on water content:

DRY FOOD vs WET FOOD

1. **Dry food**
   Dry food is the most common type of cat food that can be seen in the market or pet stores. These are also commonly termed as kibbles or pellets. As the name implies, this food type is very dry and has minimal (about 10%) to zero water content. Because of this, dry food can easily be stored and has a very long shelf-life.

If you are choosing this type of food, your cat should be drinking more water as compared to cats that are offered with wet food. It is best for the owners to check the cat's water intake when dry food is given.

2. **Wet food**

   Most wet food preparations are in aluminum and tin cans. It has a very high water content, about 70%, and can easily spoil if not stored properly after opening.

   This is best given to cats that do not drink too much water because the water content in this food type can compensate for the water that your cat does not drink. This is also recommended in certain disease conditions in cats such as constipation.

VEGETABLES

Vegetables may seldom be given to cats because cats do not get anything from vegetables except for fiber. Vegetables are often given if your cat has a disease or specific condition wherein your veterinarian will advise you when it is all right to give your cat vegetables.

It is a normal behaviour for cats to eat some vegetables and grass. Do not panic when this happens.

MILK

Be careful when you give milk to your cat especially to kittens. Cats cannot digest lactose properly that is why the milk that you drink cannot be given to your cat. Although not always, your pet cat can have diarrhea when you give it human or cow milk.

There are special pet's milk that can be given to kittens and cats. It can be bought in pet stores and veterinary clinics/hospitals. You can ask your veterinarian regarding this and other possible alternatives to cat milk.

WATER

Offer your cat fresh water daily. Always change the water in the water bowl every day. Some cats will not drink water that is not fresh especially if there is a weird smell in the water. They may look for other water sources if they don't like the water in the bowl.

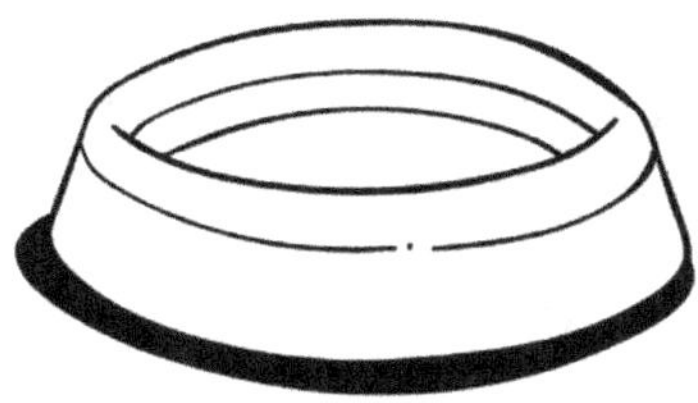

Cats' water intake will usually depend on the following:
- ✓ Type of food:
  Dry food – more water
  Wet food – less water

- ✓ Activity:
  More playful – more water
  More sleep – less water

- ✓ Weather:
  Hot season – more water
  Cold season – less water

- ✓ Sickness – depends on what condition

It is highly recommended to give your cat a big water bowl. Some cats like to drink while seeing their beautiful reflections in the water!

CAT TREATS

Cats love treats because they are usually tastier as compared to its regular cat food. They are usually given to cats when training them or when giving command. It's like a reward for them for doing a good job when it obeys its owners.

Cats love most treats because it is salty. The salt content in most treats are high as compared to your regular cat food. Frequent intake of too much salt may result in certain diseases such as kidney disease. This is why we don't give too much treats to our cats.

Just remember to only give enough cat treats. Do not give too much because they can become sick if you do so. Do not continuously give them treats even if they try to ask you by making themselves cute.

There can be many reasons why your cat does not want to eat. Your cat may not find the food delicious or it is **not familiar** with the new food. Your cat can also be **in heat** or **sick**. If you feel that this may be the case, check on your cat always.

Try offering a different type of food to your cat to see if it simply does not want its usual cat food or if it is not feeling well. When shifting to a food that is new to your cat, practice **transitional feeding** for your cat to avoid having an upset stomach which may cause vomiting and diarrhea.

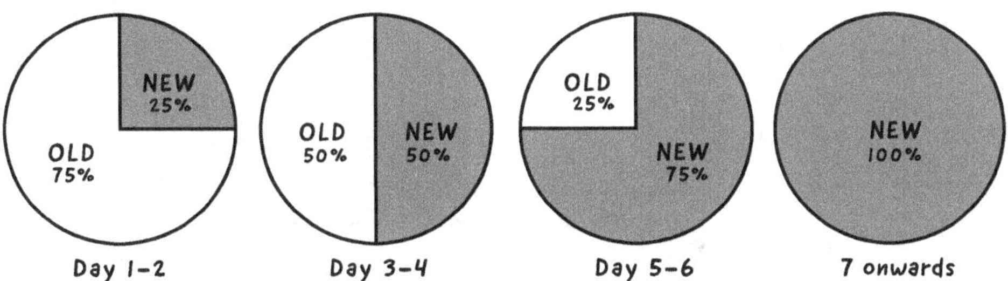

If your cat still does not want to eat even if you offer a different type of food, your cat may be sick. When this happens, bring your cat to a veterinarian for a check-up and assessment.

FOOD TO AVOID!

Cats are very sensitive pets that can easily get sick by feeding them food that are poisonous to them. When giving treats to your cats or when making homemade meals, be sure not to give or include these toxic food:

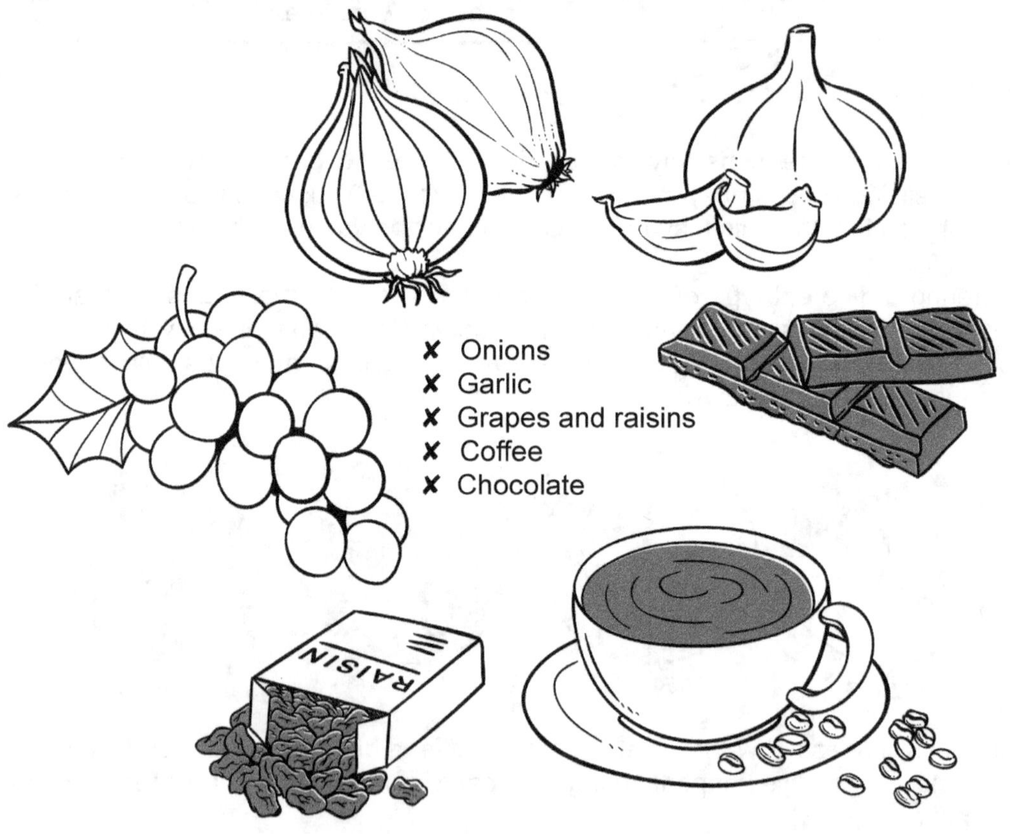

✘ Onions
✘ Garlic
✘ Grapes and raisins
✘ Coffee
✘ Chocolate

SQUEAKY CLEAN
Cat Hygiene, Bathing and Grooming

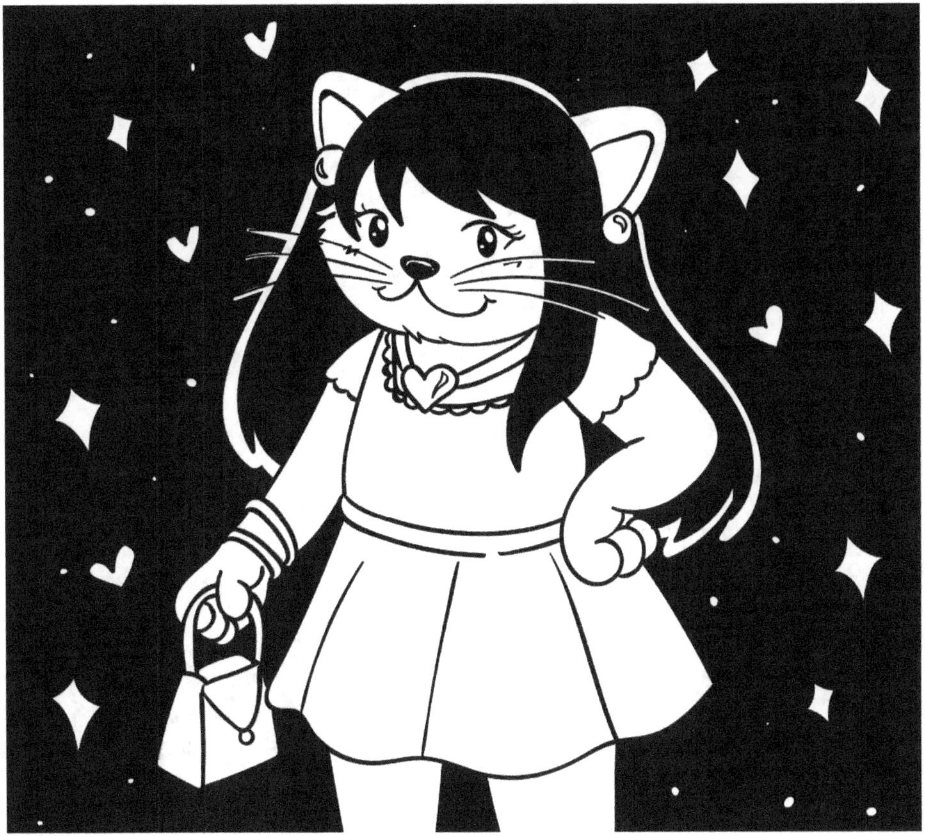

Grooming your pet cat is like you regularly taking a bath, combing your hair and trimming your nails but is less often. It keeps your cat healthier and happier. It can be a source of bonding between cats, and between you and your cat.

Cats looooooooove to groom themselves daily. However, they might need some help for their hard-to-reach places. If your cat is as fluffy as cotton, your cat may need extra grooming time.

Cats may resist grooming with their humans. **It is best to start grooming as a kitten so they get used to it.** Training them may be helpful with treats and talking in a gentle voice while grooming them.

HAIR AND COAT BRUSHING

Cats use their tongue and paws to maintain their beautiful coats. A cat's tongue has these special structures that act like a brush. With the help of their saliva, they are able to clean their head and face by wetting their paws. They then use their paws as a brush to reach them.

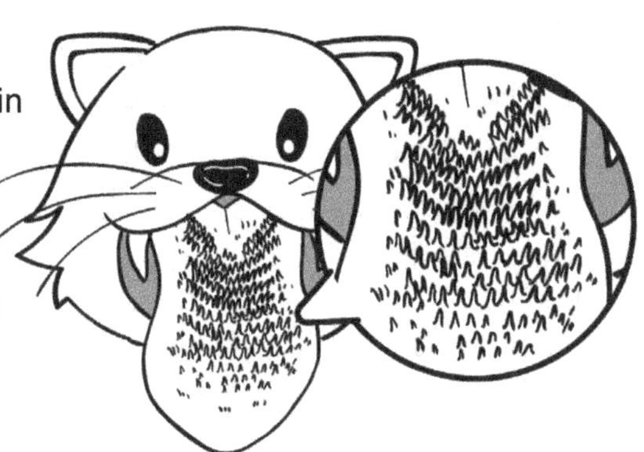

Your cat is very flexible just like an acrobat or a gymnast. It can groom itself in different positions to reach majority of their body.

Materials
- ☐ Towel (optional)
- ☐ Wide-toothed metal comb
- ☐ Rubber-bristle
  or Soft-bristle brush
- ☐ Flea (narrow-toothed)
- ☐ metal comb (optional)

Steps:

1. Stroke your cat's head repeatedly. You may wrap your cat with a towel to calm your cat at first and slowly remove the towel and pet it.

2. Use a wide-toothed comb for long-haired cats to loosen hair strands.

3. If fleas are present, use a flea comb.

4. Using a rubber or soft bristled brush, start brushing your cat's hair from the head, then to its body until its tail. Brush your cat's hair in one direction

5. Be careful when brushing their sensitive parts: **ears, armpit, belly and tail**.

Short – hair
Grooming – once to twice a month

Long – hair
Grooming – at least once a week

Short-haired cats do not need grooming as often as long-haired cats. This is because long-haired cats are prone to clumping of hair strands (matting) and hairball.

BATHING

Cats would need to take a bath when they get dirty and smelly. Since cats love to groom themselves a lot, bathing is not done frequently especially with short-haired cats. Bathing is more important for long-haired cats since they pick up more dirt because of their hair length.

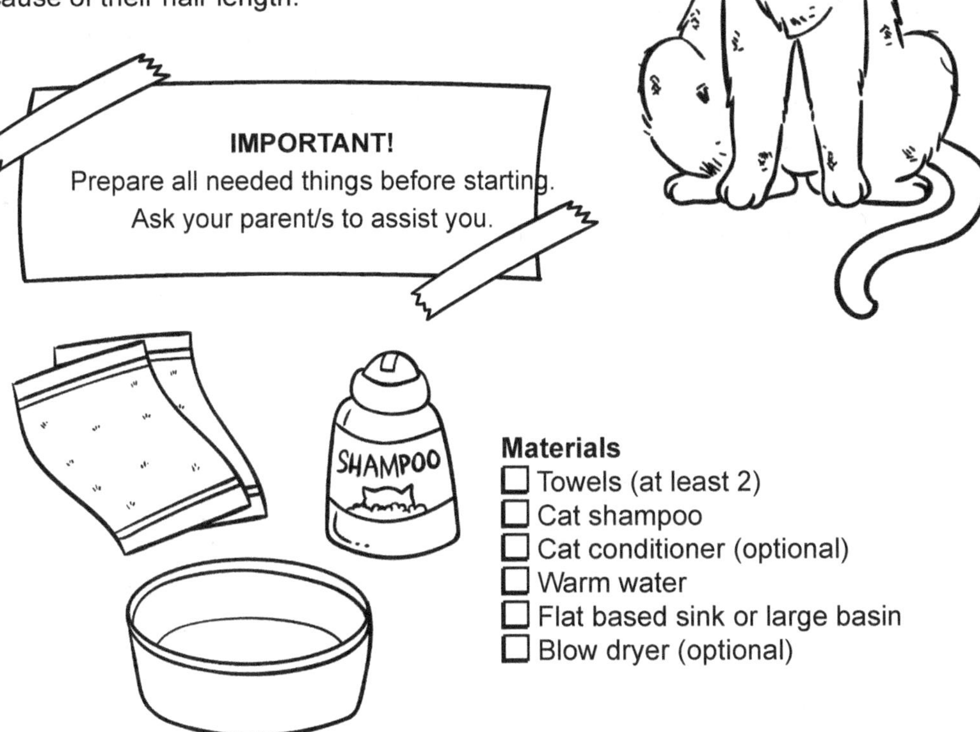

Materials
- ☐ Towels (at least 2)
- ☐ Cat shampoo
- ☐ Cat conditioner (optional)
- ☐ Warm water
- ☐ Flat based sink or large basin
- ☐ Blow dryer (optional)

Steps:

1. Place warm water inside the sink/
   basin about two (2) inches deep.

2. Test how your cat will react with the water first by placing your cat's foot one at a time. Cats may become jumpy and will try to escape. Talk to it in a gentle manner to assure that bathing is safe.

3. Wet your cat's fur slowly, apply shampoo all throughout your cat's hair and then lather. Avoid getting shampoo on the eyes, nose and mouth of your cat.

4. Rinse off the shampoo with warm water.

5. Apply conditioner on your cat's fur. Spread the conditioner with the help of a wide-toothed comb.

6. Rinse off the conditioner with warm water.

7. Gently squeeze your cat's body, legs and tail to remove water.

8. Wrap a towel around your cat.

9. Dry your cat by gently rubbing the towel wrapped around it.

10. You may use a blow dryer (cold air only) or several towels for faster drying.

Don't use a blow dryer if your cat does not like the sound of it.

> **TIP:** Most cats do not like water touching their body and taking a bath. They may panic when you bathe them. Cats are calmer when bathing if trained as early as a kitten.

USING DRY SHAMPOO

For cats that do not like taking a bath, dry shampoo will be very useful. It is like the usual bathing minus the water.

Materials
- ☐ Cat dry shampoo
- ☐ Rubber-bristle or soft-bristle brush
- ☐ Towel

Steps:
1. Apply **dry shampoo** all over your cat's body.

2. Let the shampoo stay on the cat's coat for about 10 minutes.

3. Use a rubber-bristled, soft-bristled brush or towel to remove excess shampoo.

TEETH

Cat owners often forget that the cat's teeth are also an important part of grooming. Just like what your mom would say to you: brushing your teeth prevents tooth decay. It can also help reduce serious cat infections.

Materials
- ☐ Gauze for starters
- ☐ Soft bristled toothbrush/finger toothbrush
- ☐ Flavored enzymatic toothpaste
  - • Do not use human ones
- ☐ Wet cat food (optional)

finger toothbrush

Ask your parent to help you hold your cat's head.

Steps:
1. If it is your cat's first time to have its teeth brushed, wrap your index finger with a gauze pad and apply wet cat food. If not, use the soft-bristled toothbrush or fingerbrush and apply the enzymatic flavored toothpaste.

2. Let the cat smell the cat food or toothpaste first.

3. Slowly open the cat's mouth by holding its upper head in between your thumb and four other fingers.

4. Rub the gauze pad or toothbrush against the cat's teeth to remove plaque and tartar. There is no need to rinse the toothpaste off your cat. The special toothpaste can be swallowed by your cat.

EARS

Just like you, your cat's ears may become itchy when there is accumulation of dirt in the ears. Regularly check your cat's ears if dirt accumulates in it. Be careful when cleaning your cat's ears and avoid using cotton tips/swabs.

Materials
- ☐ Soft tissue or thin cloth
- ☐ Olive or coconut oil,
    OR ear cleaning solution for pets

Steps:
1. Dip the tissue or cloth in olive or coconut oil.
2. Wipe the ear gently until you are able to remove the visible ear dirt or discharge

If there's an increase in ear discharge or if your cat easily accumulates ear dirt 2 to 3 days after ear cleaning, bring your cat to a veterinarian. This may be because of infection from bacteria, fungi or mites inside the ears of your cat.

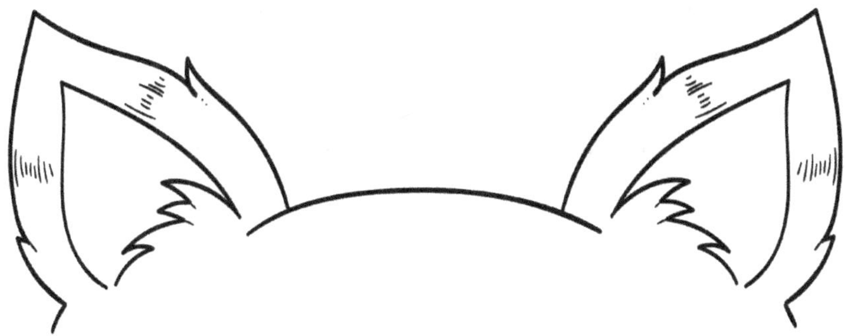

NAILS

A cat with a lot of exercise and activity does not need frequent nail trimming. Its nails are most often in contact with the floor and are usually trimmed by friction from contact with the floor.

Nail trimming can be done at least once a month. But if your cat spends most of its time outdoors, do not trim its nails too much because the nail or its claw is part of your cat's protection and defense against possible wild animals that may attack it. Nail trimming might not be even necessary for an outdoor cat.

Steps:

1. Visualize the appearance of your cat's claw first. You will be able to see a transparent part and a pink part. The pink area has the blood supply for the nail.

2. Cut at the transparent part before the pink area (see the dashed line).

3. Avoid the pink area because cutting it will make the nail bleed.

4. In case of bleeding, use a cotton and press the area that is bleeding.

If you are not sure about trimming your cat's nails yourself, bring your cat to a grooming center or veterinarian.

REMINDER! ALWAYS HAVE YOUR PARENT/S ASSIST YOU! NYA~

Chapter 7

TOILET ETIQUETTE
Training Your Cat to Use Its Litter Box

Using the litter box is one of the cat's natural behaviours as they treat this box as their toilet. You may follow these easy steps in preparing and handling your cat's litter box.

PREPARING AND CLEANING THE LITTER TRAY

1. Place the litter box away from your cat's feeding and sleeping area. This should be placed preferably in a quiet area where people seldom go (e.g. dirty kitchen, near toilet). This is because cats can be easily disturbed by loud noises when they poo and urinate.

2. Put your litter material (See page 20 for the different types of litter material) inside the box until you have approximately 2 inches deep of the material.

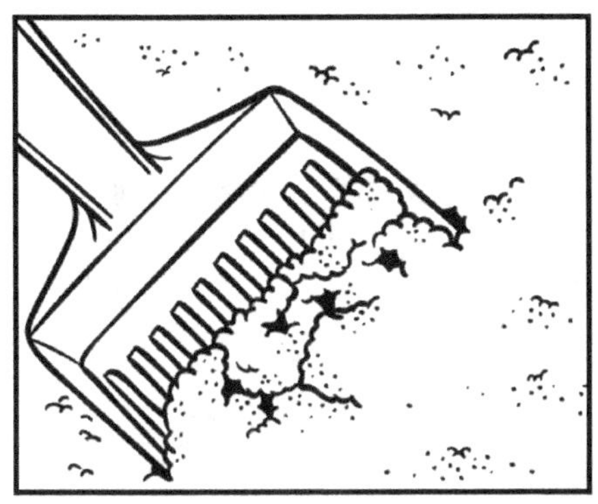

3. When your cat urinates or poops, the litter material will clump, if you use a clumping litter material. Remove these clumps daily using a litter scoop. You can either flush, throw or bury the clumps depending on the material that you are using. Provide a separate container to throw away urine and poop clumps.

4. Do not forget to thoroughly clean your hands after doing preparing or cleaning the litter tray.

5. Replace the whole litter material, even if unused, once every 1 to 2 weeks.

Because of their innate hygienic nature, cats tend to instantly learn their way around a litter box. Kittens, on the other hand, may need some teaching and guidance for potty training from you, its owner, although if the mother cat is there to teach them, thats fine too. When kittens reach about a month or so, they may need to start training to use the litter box.

1. To train your kitten to use the litter box, bring your kitten to the litter box about 10 to 15 minutes after a meal.

2. Hold its front paws and let them feel the sand by digging into it. You may have to repeat this action until the kitten learns that the litter box is a place to urinate and poo.

3. If the kitten fails to use the litter box, try to pick up its poop and place it on the sand.

4. Bring your kitten to the litter box, let it smell the poop and teach them to dig into the sand to cover the poop.

Once a cat has been trained to use its litter box, it will be using its litter box to urinate and defecate for the rest of its life. However, when a cat is sick, it has a tendency to urinate or defecate anywhere outside the litter box. This is one way for them to tell their owners that they are sick and it is about time to bring them to a veterinarian.

Chapter 8

HOW TO CAT?
Behaviour, Traits and Attitude

Your cat buddy is a highly independent and intelligent pet. However, unlike dogs, a cat doesn't like taking commands. This is the reason why it is more difficult to train them.

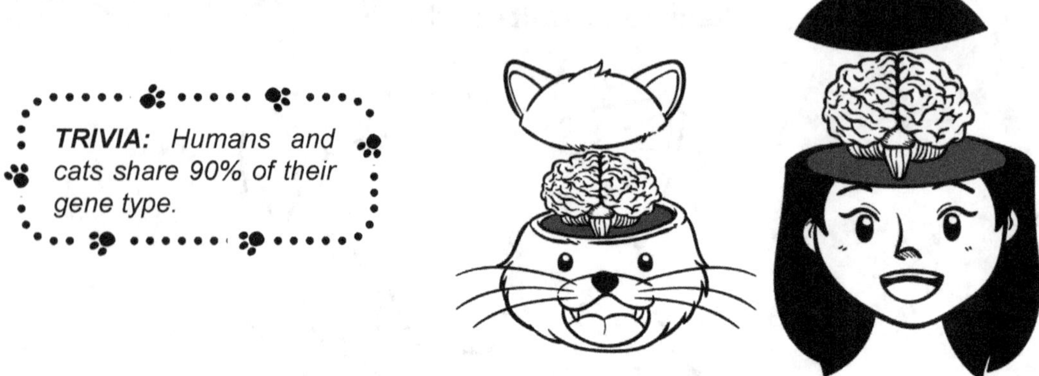

Their behaviour is different as compared to dogs and may be a little hard to understand at first. A very good example of this is the wagging of its tail. In dogs, it means that the dog is very happy and content. With cats, it may mean that it is upset and mad.

Familiarizing yourself on how your cat acts, behaves and communicates will let you know your cat more and be aware if there is something wrong with your cat.

COMMUNICATION

A cat's "meow" can mean different things depending on its pitch.

Purr   – means your cat is contented
Hiss or – means your cat
snarl   is angry or scared
Chitter – means your cat
              is excited and curious

TRIVIA: Siamese cats are some of the most talkative cats!

Talking to your cat in a gentle manner is comforting to them. Cats may react differently depending on how you, as its owner, talk to them.

A high pitched voice will be reassuring for them and may mean that you like what they are doing. On the other hand, a low pitched voice may mean that the owner is mad at them. These voice pitches may help the owner in disciplining their cats. See Chapter 12 on steps on how you can discipline your cat.

Cats respond more often to the person the cat has most contact with and is close to since they were a kitten. When used to, the cat will only respond with only one name in a certain pitch. That is why it is not advisable to call your cat different names.

BODY LANGUAGE

You can also understand how your cat feels by its body language.

<u>EYES</u>

- Dilate – may indicate fear; observed during night time

- Narrow slits pupils – may indicate aggressiveness and stress; observed during day time.

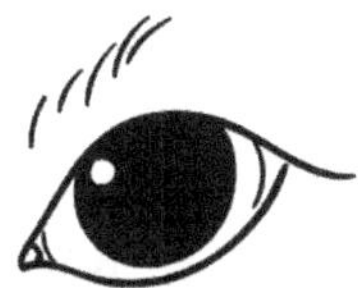

<u>EARS</u>

- Ears pointing backward (airplane ears) – scared

- Ears pointing downward – ready to attack

- Ears pointing forward – friendly, playful, curious

- Fur stands
  – ready to attack or fear

- Exposing belly – trust

- Wagging its tail is not
  the same in dogs – angry

- **Kneading**
  - behaviour maintained as a kitten
  - kneading mother cat's breast when drinking milk
  - satisfied, relaxed, about to sleep

- **Tail upward (curved)**
  - curious, playful

- **Tail downward/hiding in between legs – scared**

TRIVIA: When a cat blinks its eyes slowly in front of you, it means that it trusts you. You may try doing the same action when you see your cat doing this.

TERRITORIAL

Marking its territory is very prominent in almost all pets. It is their way of telling other animals or pets that a certain area or object is theirs. This behaviour is more common in males than females.

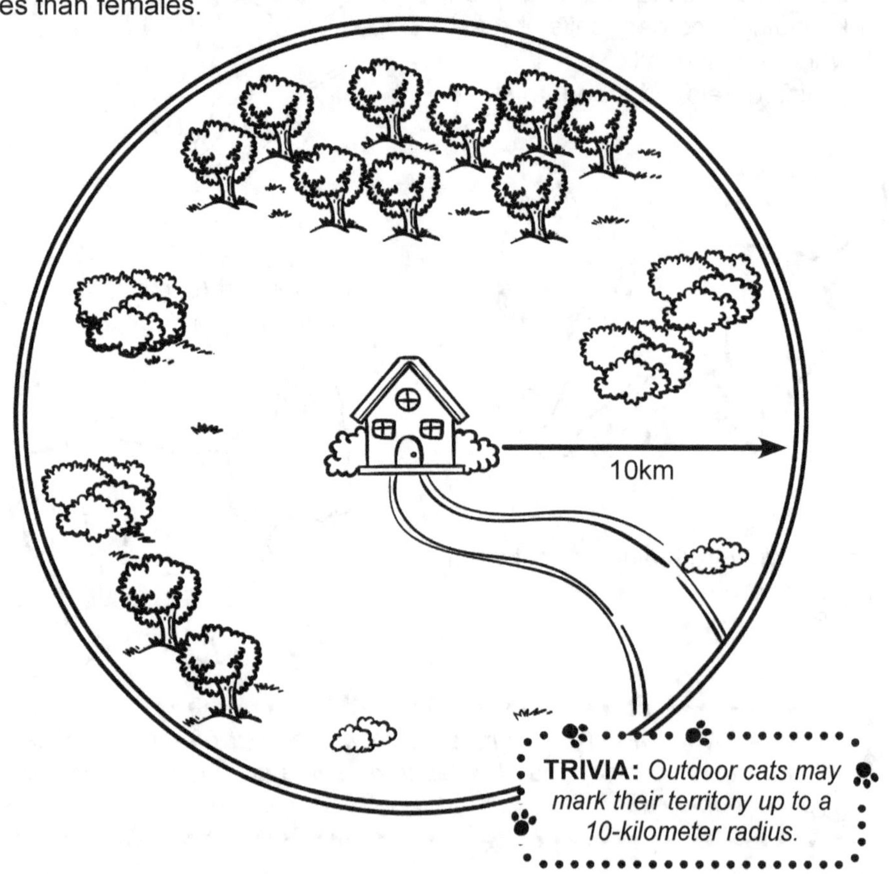

Cats mark their territory in two common ways. They either spray urine or rub their bodies against furniture and the floor.

When cats rub their bodies against objects, they make use of special glands and neck that release a scent on their marked object.

This type of behaviour may be difficult to manage especially if you have many cats at home and if they are not yet neutered.

Neutering may help reduce this behaviour. See **Chapter 10** for more information about **neutering**.

AGGRESSIVENESS and STRESS

Cats may become aggressive if they are scared, annoyed, stressed or sick. This behaviour is usually observed when a cat encounters another cat or pet, and when visiting the veterinarian. When this happens, especially when your cat is annoyed, let it relax first on its own and try talking to your cat in a calm and gentle voice.

Do not continue annoying your cat once it becomes aggressive. Cats are very prone to stress that may result in your cat becoming sick.

Common factors that may stress your cat:
✓ Sudden change in environment:
   arrangement of furniture,
   feeding bowls and litter box
✓ New pet at home
✓ Very noisy environment
   (ex. construction in a nearby area)

Chapter 9

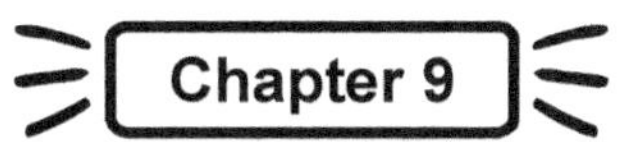

HEALTH IS WEALTH

Keeping Your Cat Healthy

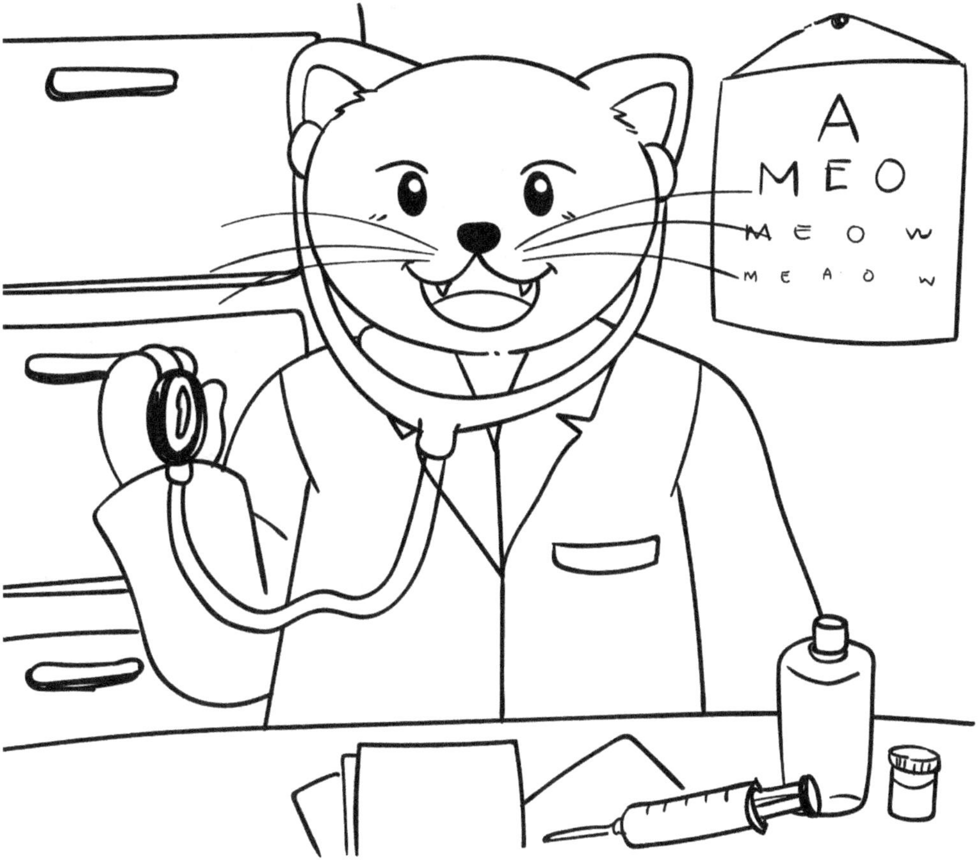

A healthy cat will have shiny hair, bright eyes with no discharge, nose that is slightly moist, pink gums and free from parasites on its body.

Keeping your cat healthy is as easy as pie with the correct nutrition, feeding, environment and preventives.

Preventives are medicines or drugs that are given to your cat on a regular basis for them to avoid being sick. Examples of which are vaccines, deworming and flea treatments.

VACCINES, DEWORMING, AND FLEA PREVENTIVES

There are several ways to protect your pal from some serious cat diseases such as rabies. Regular vaccination and deworming will ensure that your cat is protected from diseases brought by viruses and worms.

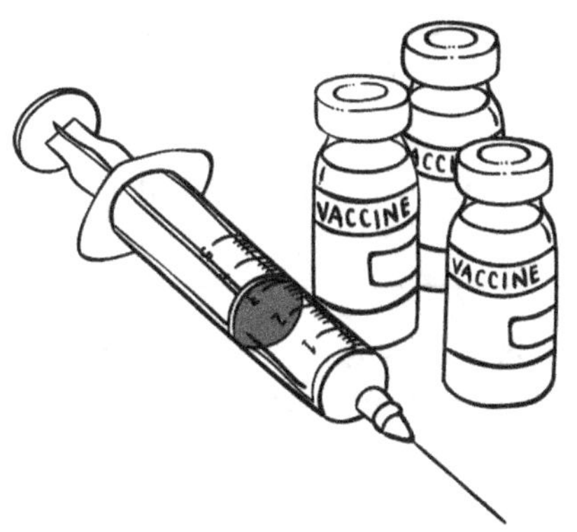

Deworming is usually done to prevent your cat from acquiring worms from other cats or the environment. However, it can also be done as treatment if your cat is already infected with worms.

There are two types of vaccines that may be given to your cat: a multi-core vaccine and a rabies vaccine.

A multi-core vaccine protects your cat from different types of viruses and bacteria such as Feline Panleukopenia Virus, which can be deadly in cats. Most multi-core vaccines will protect cats from at least two types of diseases.

Between the two vaccines, rabies vaccine can be considered more important because of its potential effect to humans. However, both vaccines are highly recommended for your cat especially if your cat will have access outdoors.

Lastly, flea preventives can also be given to your cat depending on the weight and age of the animal. You may consult your veterinarian regarding this matter.

Use the table below to know when it's best for your cat to get vaccinated and dewormed.

Vaccination and Deworming Schedule

Minimum Age	What to do?	Notes
2 weeks old	Deworming	To be given every 2 weeks for 3 to 4 sessions/time. Repeated every 3 (outdoor) to 6 (indoor) months.
6 weeks old	Multi-core Vaccination	After the first shot, another shot is given after 3-4 weeks. Repeated once every year.
12 weeks old	Rabies Vaccination	Once every year
	Flea preventive	Consult your veterinarian for options

* Different veterinary clinics and hospitals might have different vaccination and deworming scheduling. Ask your veterinarian what schedule and preventives might be best for your cat.

Once your cat has been vaccinated, a record book and/or certificate will be provided by your veterinarian. Never lose this and keep it in a safe place. Always remember to bring this every time you visit a veterinarian.

CHECK-UPS

Cats that are more than 10 years old are already considered senior cats. It is recommended that your senior cat visits your veterinarian more regularly as compared to your younger cats. They have to be brought to the hospital once every 6 months routine check of its general condition which may include the liver, heart and kidneys.

"HELP, I AM SICK!"

Sick cats, just like their ancestors in the wild, are very good in pretending that they don't have any disease. By doing this, they protect themselves from possible predators in the wild.

To know if your cat is sick, you should know your cat's attitude and behaviour well: how it eats, plays, and acts. If these behaviours change, your cat might be sick.

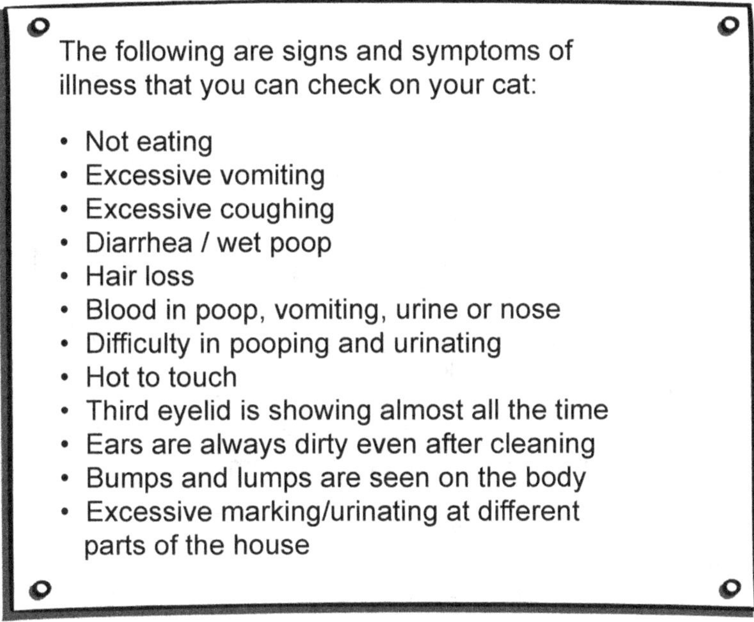

If your cat shows at least one of the symptoms on the list, it is best to bring your cat to a veterinarian for a check-up.

An early check-up when your cat is sick prevents the disease from becoming serious or life-threatening.

COMMON DISEASES AND POSSIBLE CAUSES

Specific signs and symptoms may give you an idea about what is going on with your cat. There is no single sign or symptom that can immediately indicate a specific cat disease.

Below are some examples of signs and symptoms that you may observe in your cat with its corresponding possible causes:

- **Excessive vomiting** – hairball, ingested foreign object, intestinal worms
- **Diarrhea and blood in poop** – intestinal worms, bacterial infection
- **Hair loss** – fungal infection, scabies, fleas
- **Urine straining or blood in urine** – infection, kidney or urinary stones, kidney problem
- **Coughing** – pneumonia, heart problem
- **Ear discharge** – bacteria or fungal infection, ear mites
- **Bumps and lumps** - abscess, tumor

If you are unsure of your sick cat's sign and symptoms, it is best to consult your veterinarian for proper medication and management of your cat. Do not try to self-medicate your sick cat, if possible. Treating your cat on your own may cause more problems to your cat.

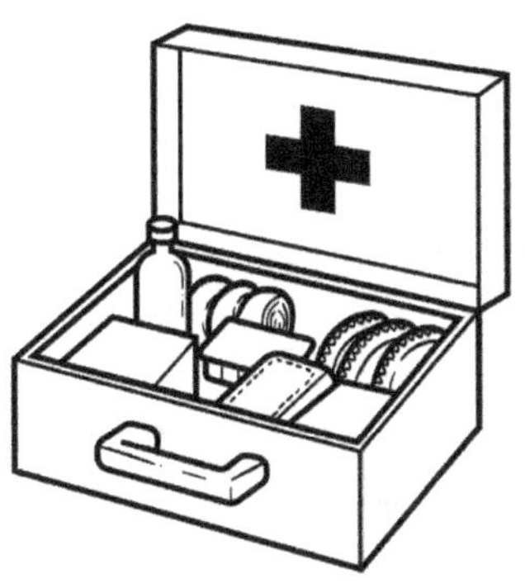

FIRST AID

Minor injuries and sickness such as small wounds can be addressed at your home with easily available supplies. However, if you are unsure if your cat's injury is minor or not, consult your veterinarian.

WOUNDS

Small wounds from cat fights and other objects can be initially managed by cleaning and disinfecting your cat's wound. You may use a **gauze** and **10% povidone iodine** which can be easily bought in most drugstores. Simply clean the area with the povidone iodine and leave an amount of it on the wound. This can be done daily for five days.

If the wound is observed to be healing on the third day, you may opt not to bring your cat to the veterinarian. However, if it looks like it is not healing on the third day and seems to be infected and deep, bring your cat to the veterinarian immediately.

NOT EATING

A cat that does not eat for a day or two can be normal. (See page 43). During this time, you may prepare a homemade sugar solution for your cat by mixing 3 tbsp. of table sugar in 10 mL water.

However, if you observe that your cat has not been eating for about three days already, this first aid will not help your cat anymore. It might need medical attention already and its best to bring it to a veterinary hospital.

Keep in mind that cats are great in hiding their illnesses. Do not delay your cat's visit to a veterinarian if an abnormal behaviour has been observed for three days already.

Chapter 10

NEUTERING
Cat Population Control

Neutering is defined as the removal of an animal's reproductive organ/s. Other terms that are used to describe and define this word are sterilization, fixing, castration (for male cats) and spaying (for female cats). This procedure is done under general anesthesia.

WHY NEUTER?

The main reason for neutering cats and dogs is to avoid excessive and unwanted future pregnancies that may result in a number of kittens that the owner may have a hard time taking care of. This allows control of cat population within an area.

There are also several reasons and benefits why this procedure is done. Territorial behaviour may be lessened when a cat has been neutered. They tend to be more relaxed and chill after the procedure. Aggressiveness may also be decreased significantly by neutering.

Neutering is very beneficial to both owners and their pets. However, pet owners have to be aware of the negative effects of neutering to some pets. Your cat's ability to use up the nutrients it gets from food or metabolism could also be decreased by neutering them. Because of this, neutered cats have a tendency to gain weight and become obese. To avoid this, it is recommended to play more with a neutered cat, and give it just the right amount and kind of food.

Cats, regardless of their sex, can be neutered as early as 6 months of age just about the time they become sexually matured to reproduce offspring.

Male cats are easier to neuter as compared to female cats. Therefore, female cats need more post-operative (after surgery) care and may need to be a little older prior to neutering.

It is best to talk or visit your veterinarian personally with your cat for the veterinarian to assess if your cat is fit for surgery. Blood tests may be done prior to surgery to ensure that your cat is healthy and strong enough to undergo surgery.

Your veterinarian will either perform the surgery on the same day blood tests are done or schedule a surgery date for your pet.

Different veterinary clinics and hospitals may have their own scheduling and procedure when neutering. This is why you need to talk to your veterinarian prior to getting your cat neutered.

POST-OPERATIVE CARE

As a general rule, cats that have undergone surgeries need to be isolated and looked after at home for a few days. Medications and wound management may be advised by your veterinarian depending on your cat's needs.

It is normal for some cats to be lethargic after surgery but only for the first day. Most cats will immediately be back to their usual activities right after the anesthesia has worn off.

Male cats that underwent castration need very minimal care. There are no stitches done on male cats and owners are usually advised to check for swelling of the surgical site.

Female cats need more attention and care after sugery. More medications and wound management is given to them.

Chapter 11

CAT ADOPTION
Helping Abandoned Cats Find Their Fur-ever Homes

Cats make great pets. However, some cats are continuously being abandoned in shelters and even left on the streets. The common reasons for abandoning cats are the increasing number of cats in a household and the inability of a person to take care of a cat.

This is why an individual and his/her family should be prepared and fully aware of the responsibilities of taking care of a cat prior to getting one. In addition, neutering (see **Chapter 10**) can greatly reduce the number of abandoned cats by controlling unwanted cat pregnancies within the household.

Shelter Adoption

If one is ready to take care of a cat, adopting from a shelter is one option to get a new cat. Adopting a cat from a shelter is like saving a cat's life. You are allowing an abandoned cat to experience a better life that is full of love and care. You are letting them find their fur-ever homes with you.

How to take care of an abandoned/adopted kitten

Unlike abandoned or adopted adult cats, abandoned or adopted kittens, especially those that are not independent yet, need much attention. They cannot eat, drink or even urinate and defecate on their own yet.

Below are the ways on how you should take care of an abandoned or adopted kitten.

Feeding:
- [ ] Cat/Pet milk, powdered or ready-to-drink
- [ ] Bottle feeder for cats
  OR 1-mL syringe (remove needle)

1. Buy pet milk from a pet store or veterinary clinic.
2. Prepare a powdered cat milk according to its label's instructions.
3. Feed the kitten with milk every one to two hours using a cat bottle feeder or a 1-mL syringe.
4. When feeding the kittens, please take note of the proper position of the kitten's body and head.

This is the proper way
to feed kittens with milk
to avoid the milk from
going inside the kitten's lungs.

Urination and Defecation

Kittens under two-weeks of age need a stimulus to urinate and defecate. This is possible when a mother cat licks the kitten's genitals after meals. But because abandoned kittens usually do not have a mother cat to do this, you as the owner have to mimic this behaviour using a moist cotton.

You will need:
- [ ] Cotton
- [ ] Water

1. Moist the cotton with water without getting it dripping wet.

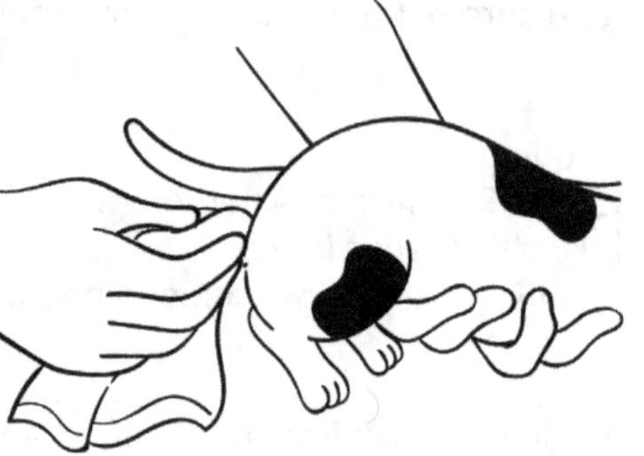

2. Ten to fifteen minutes after feeding the kitten, wipe the kitten's genitals and anus to mimic the mother cat's licking behaviour.

3. Continue doing this until kitten is able to

defecate and urinate.

TRY THESE AT HOME
Different Do-It-Yourself (DIY) Activities

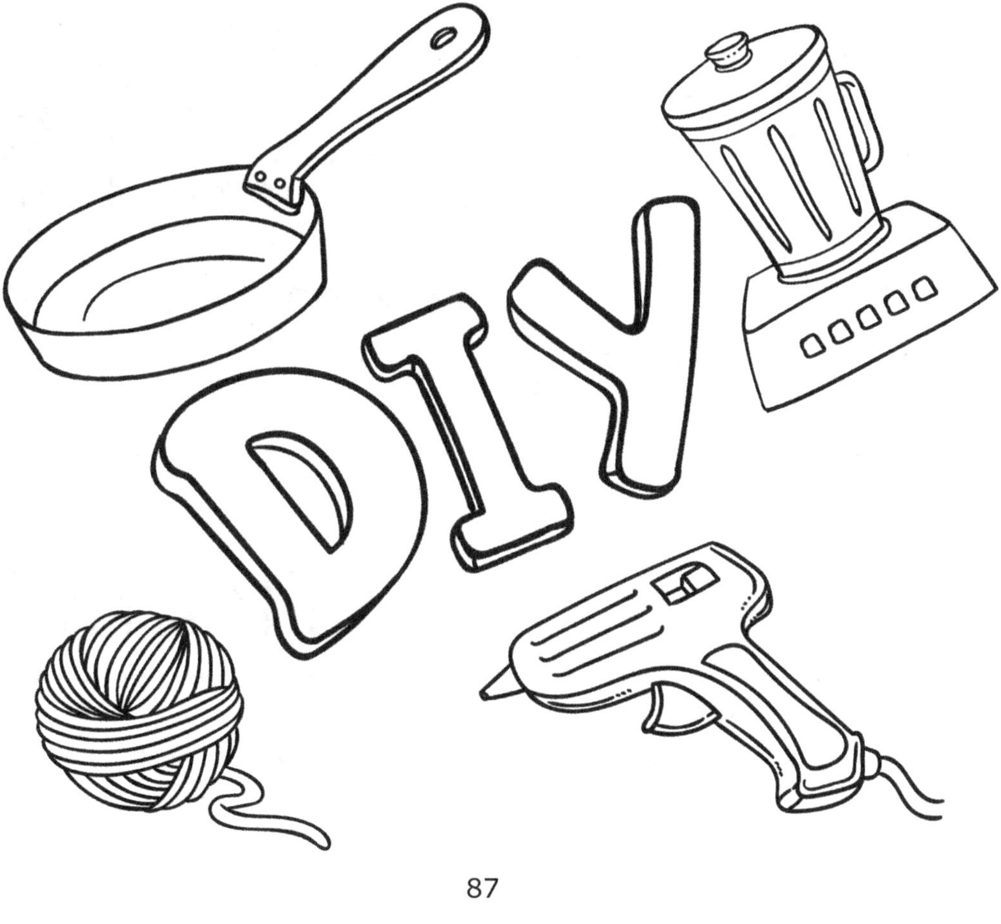

Congratulations! You've reached this chapter of the book! You are now fully equipped with the knowledge on how you can properly take care of your cat. But, it does not end there! There are extra things that you and your cat can do for additional bonding and fun.

In this chapter, you will learn how to make homemade cat food, treats and toys. You can create something personal that will make your cat feel special.

These are just some examples and you may ask your veterinarian for other recipes or materials.

There are also fun activities and basic commands included that you can teach your cat.

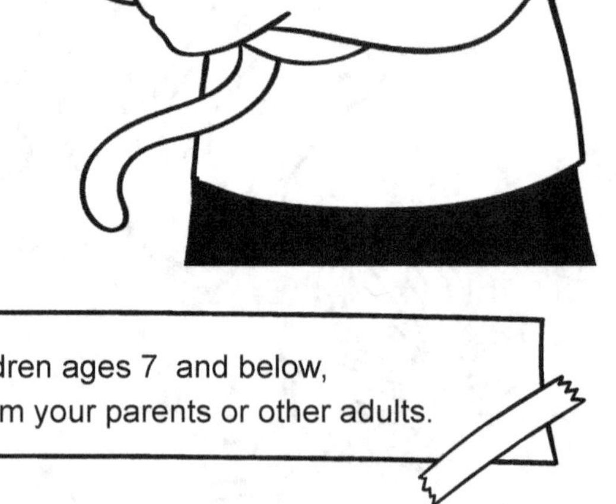

IMPORTANT: For children ages 7 and below, be sure that you have help from your parents or other adults.

CAT FOOD RECIPES FOR DIFFERENT AGES

Kitten

Ingredients:
- ☐ ½ kilo Chicken breast, skin removed
- ☐ 1 cup White rice, cooked
- ☐ 5 tbsp. Canola oil
- ☐ ¼ tsp. Salt
- ☐ 4 ½ tsp. Bone meal powder
  (available in agricultural/poultry supply shops)
- ☐ 3 tablets Multivitamins and minerals for adults (available in drugstores)
- ☐ ½ of 1,000-mg Taurine tablet (available in drugstores)

Steps:
1. Boil chicken in water until cooked.

2. Once cooked, set aside to cool down.

3. After cooling, cut the chicken into little pieces. This can be shredded or sliced.

4. Mix chicken, cooked rice, oil, salt, bone meal powder, pulverized vitamins and taurine tablets.

5. Keep in a dry plastic container for future meals.

6. Store inside the refrigerator or freezer.

Good for at least 5 meals.

Adult Cat

Ingredients:
☐ 400 grams Chicken breast, skin removed
☐ 1 ½ cup White rice, cooked,
☐ 5 tbsp. Canola oil,
☐ ¼ tsp. Salt
☐ 2 ½ tsp. Bone meal powder
   (available in agricultural/poultry supply shops)
☐ 3 tablets Multivitamins and minerals (available in drugstores)
☐ ½ of 1,000-mg Taurine tablet, (available in drugstores)

Steps:

1. Boil chicken in water until cooked.

2. Once cooked, set aside to cool down.

3. After cooling, cut the chicken into little pieces. This can be shredded or sliced

4. Mix chicken, cooked rice, oil, salt, bone meal powder, pulverized vitamins and taurine tablet.

5. Keep in a dry plastic container for future meals.

6. Store inside the refrigerator or freezer.

Good for at least 5 meals.

Senior/Old Cat

Ingredients:
- ☐ 300 grams Chicken, skin removed
- ☐ 1 cup White rice, cooked
- ☐ 3 tbsp. Canola oil
- ☐ ¼ tsp. Salt
- ☐ 2 tsp. Bone meal powder (available in agricultural/poultry supply shops)
- ☐ 1 ½ tablet Multivitamins and minerals (available in drugstores)
- ☐ ½ of 1000-mg Taurine tablet (available in drugstores)

Steps:
1. Boil chicken in water until cooked.

2. Once cooked, set aside to cool down.

3. After cooling, cut the chicken into little pieces. This can be shredded or sliced

4. Mix chicken, cooked rice, oil, salt, bone meal powder, pulverized vitamins and taurine tablets.

5. Keep in a dry plastic container for future meals.

6. Store inside the refrigerator or freezer.

Good for at least 5 meals.

Chicken or Beef Jerky Treat

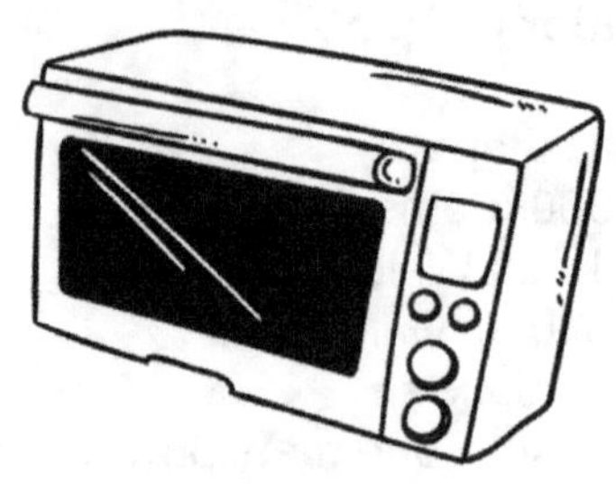

Ingredients:
- [ ] Chicken breast or beef brisket or flank
- [ ] Pinch of salt
- [ ] Cooking Oil

Steps:
1. Preheat oven on lowest setting.

2. Slice meat into approximately 1/8 inch strips.

3. Remove oven racks and apply oil on them.

4. Place foil at the bottom of the oven for the drippings.

5. Put meat strips horizontally on the rack, with approximately ½ inch space between the meat.

6. Place rack back into the oven and bake meat for about 3 hours with the oven door slightly ajar. You are not necessarily cooking the meat but drying it out for longer shelf life.

7. Cool jerky and store in a cool and dark place. This may be stored for about a year if dried properly.

TOYS and OTHER SUPPLIES

PUFFBALL

Materials:
☐ Yarn, any color
☐ Scissors

Steps:

1. Wrap yarn around your index, middle, ring,
    and little finger for about 15 times.

2. Remove the yarn from your fingers and
    tie around the middle of your yarn layers.

3. Cut the yarn on both ends to produce
    a puff-like yarn ball.

4. Your cat may now play with its puff ball.

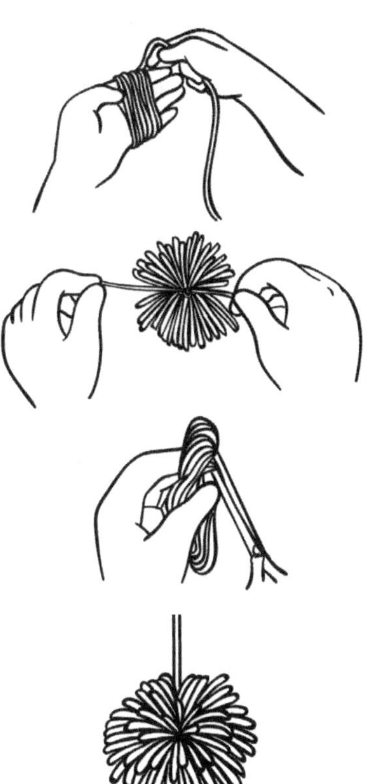

TOY WAND

Materials:
- ☐ Puffball (to make your own, see page 93)
- ☐ Yarn
- ☐ Needle with big hole (for yarn)
- ☐ Wooden stick
- ☐ Rubber band (optional)
- ☐ Glue gun with glue sticks
- ☐ Scissors

Steps:

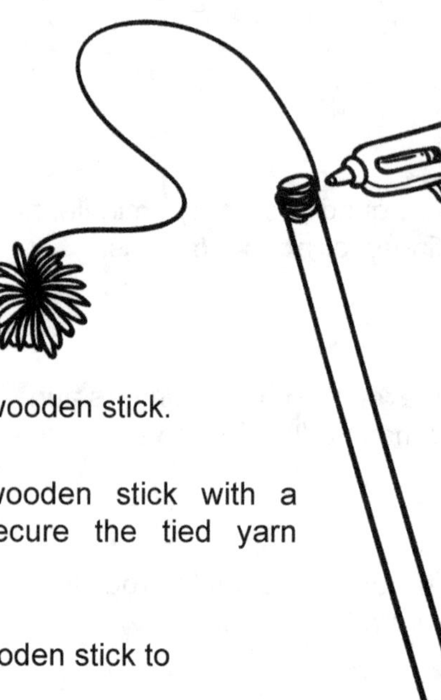

1. Sew a long yarn on a puffball.

2. Tie the long yarn at the end of the wooden stick.

3. Secure the tied yarn on the wooden stick with a rubber band if you want to secure the tied yarn even more.

4. Apply glue at the tied end of the wooden stick to secure your threads and bands.

5. Once secured, you can now use it to play with your cat.

TOY PUZZLE

Materials:
- ☐ Old plastic bottle, small
- ☐ Cutter
- ☐ Scissors
- ☐ Cat Treats

Steps:

1. Clean and dry an old plastic bottle.

2. With the help of an adult, make several holes on the body of the bottle using your cutter and/or scissors. Holes should be almost the same size as your cat treat.

3. Place cat treats inside the bottle and cover the bottle.

4. Let your cat roll and play with the bottle to get the treat outside the bottle through the holes.

PET BED

Materials:

- [ ] Old sweater
- [ ] Old pillows
- [ ] Scissors
- [ ] Yarn
- [ ] Large needle, for yarn

Steps:

1. Close the collar and neck of the sweater by sewing them with a blanket stitch.

2. Sew the chest area with a running stitch from the right armpit to the left armpit.

3. Stuff the bottom half with an old pillow and close the edge with a blanket stitch.

4. Place pillow stuffing inside the sleeves until they become fluffy enough for your cat.

5. Insert the end of one sleeve inside the other sleeve and sew them together.

Your cat bed is now ready to use!

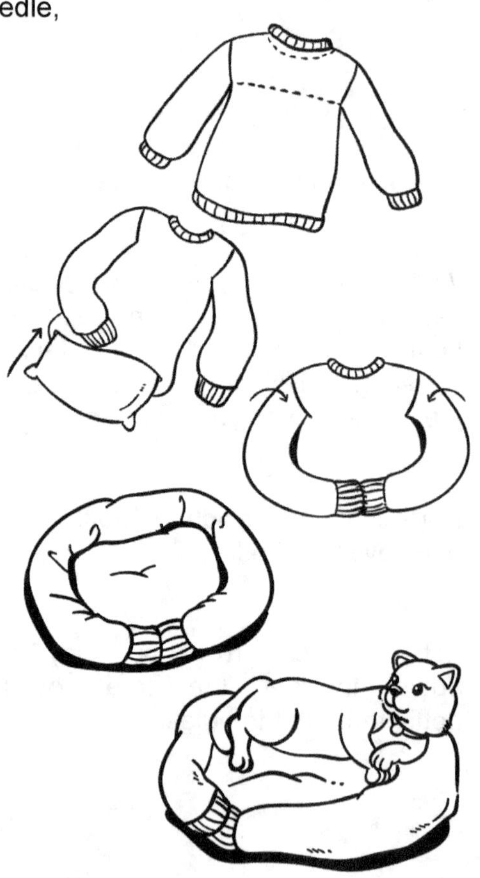

TRICKS AND COMMANDS FOR YOUR CAT

Cats are very smart pets. They can be disciplined and taught a few tricks. Unfortunately, unlike dogs, cats do not like taking commands.

You may discipline your cat in lots of ways but here are a few tips for you to start with:

- When scolding a cat, a light tap on your cat's nose while saying "NO" in a low pitched voice may suffice. The pitch of your voice and the action done will allow your cat to establish that what he was just doing is disliked by the owner.

Disciplining your cat:
NO! With a light tap on nose
(low pitched voice)

- When praising a cat, talk to your cat in a high pitched voice while saying "Good boy/girl/cat." You may stroke and scratch its head in a gentle manner. Cats like this action a lot which allows them to repeat the action they had previously done that made you praise them.

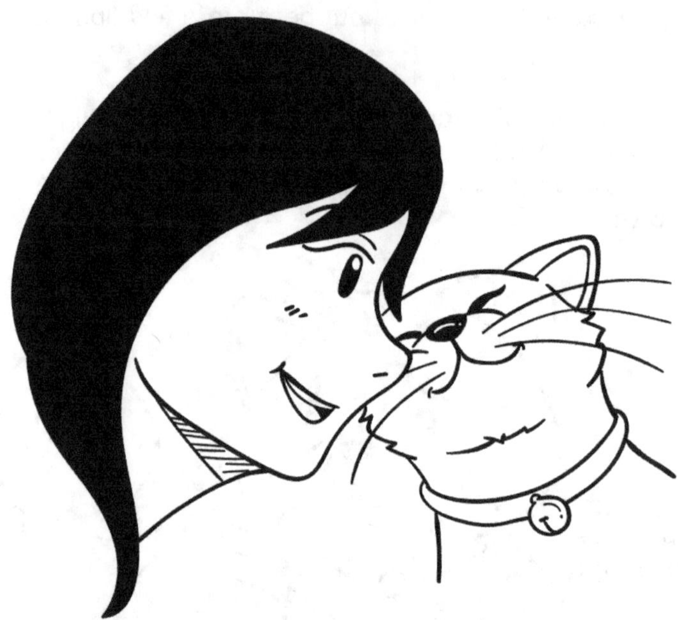

The key to training your cat for tricks and commands is rewarding them with cat treats. You may also offer your cat a treat whenever you try to praise it with good behaviour.

Acknolwedgment

The author would like to extend her gratitude to the following people who've been of great help to the development of this book: fellow vet doctors Jed dela Cruz and Dana Decena.

The production of this book would not have been possible without the trust of Ms. Ruth Catabijan of St. Matthew's Publishing Corporation. I was thrilled when she asked me to produce a book with them on taking care of cats. I have always wanted to educate more people, especially kids, because cats are often misunderstood and are not treated the right way. This has been one of my life goals. Through this book, I hope to encourage more people to consider cats as pets and especially adopt one from shelters.

Most importantly, I would like to give my enormous gratitude and appreciation to my sister and illustrator of this book, Sol Racho. I have been one of her biggest fans since we were kids and never thought twice of making her the illustrator of this book. Who could have imagined two sisters working together to produce a book for a pet that they both love?

Bibliography

Edwards, Alan. The Ultimate Encylcopedia of Cats, Cat Breeds and Cat Care. USA: Lorenz Books, 1999

Pintera, Albert. The Illustrated Guide to Cats. Translated by Eva Klimentova. London: Chancellor Press,1993.

Schenck, Patricia. Home-Prepared Dog and Cat Diets. USA: Wiley-Blackwell, 2010.

About the Author

Dr. Ma. Rosario, or Doc Rio, to those who know her well, is a veterinarian from the University of the Philippines Los Baños, and a proud owner of eight cats and four dogs. She was not a cat person to begin with but fell totally in love with them almost as soon as she got her first cat, and she has loved all her cats ever since. Her love and passion for dogs and cats motivated her to take up veterinary medicine and has taken pleasure in treating sick dogs and cats as a companion animal practitioner.

www.ingramcontent.com/pod-product-compliance
Lightning Source LLC
Chambersburg PA
CBHW060120120726
48003CB00009B/2724